SPEAK THE WORLD

Italian

History & Culture Through Language

SPEAK THE WORLD

Italian

History & Culture Through Language

MARGHERITA BERTI, PhD, FOUNDER OF @ITALIANMATTERS

ADAMS MEDIA
New York Amsterdam/Antwerp London Toronto
Sydney/Melbourne New Delhi

adamsmedia

Adams Media
An Imprint of Simon & Schuster, LLC
100 Technology Center Drive
Stoughton, MA 02072

First Adams Media hardcover edition
August 2026

Interior design by Maya Caspi
Interior images © 123RF; Getty Images; Adobe Stock

Manufactured in the United States of America

1 2026

Library of Congress Control Number: 2026939103

ISBN 978-1-5072-2631-5
ISBN 978-1-5072-2632-2 (ebook)

To my husband, thank you for your constant support, patience, and belief in me, *ti amo*.

To my boys, you are the reason behind everything I do, and the joy that keeps me going every day.

To my parents, thank you for grounding me, encouraging me, and inspiring me.

And to anyone chasing a dream, this is for you.

Contents

Introduction

Why say "hello" when you can greet someone with a *ciao* or a warm *buongiorno*? Why settle for "I'm excited" when *non vedo l'ora* says it with so much more feeling? Italian doesn't just communicate, it expresses. It adds color, warmth, and rhythm to the everyday.

Speak the World: Italian invites you to discover Italy through its language, one word and phrase at a time. Each expression in this book tells a small but important story. A toast isn't just raised; it's shared with a smile and a *cin cin*. Dinner doesn't simply begin; it comes alive when someone calls out, *A tavola!* These aren't just words. They reflect what matters most in Italian life: connection, community, and beauty in the simple things. Learning Italian is about much more than memorizing vocabulary. It's an invitation to experience a way of life.

This book introduces two hundred essential words and expressions that go beyond grammar to reveal the soul of Italy. Designed for travelers, heritage speakers, and anyone drawn to the language of art, food, and love, it offers a meaningful way to connect more deeply with Italian culture. You'll uncover:

- Everyday expressions like *fare una passeggiata* ("to take a walk")
- Cultural gems like *dolce far niente* ("the sweetness of doing nothing")
- Warm greetings like *baci e abbracci* ("hugs and kisses")
- And much more!

The journey begins with Chapter 1 and a brief look at where the Italian language comes from, how it has evolved, and how it's spoken today. Then, in Chapter 2, you'll discover a simple pronunciation guide to help you feel confident speaking the language aloud. From there, the heart of the book unfolds across four themed chapters: Greetings, Farewells, and Conversations; Food and Fun; Family and Traditions; and Idioms and Colloquialisms. Each entry within these themes includes pronunciation, part of speech, an English translation, and a short cultural insight that explains not just what the word or phrase means, but why Italians use it. Some expressions are tied to food, others to emotion, family, or local pride, but all help you understand more than just Italian grammar.

By the end of this book, you won't just recognize Italian words; you'll understand how language shapes culture, connection, and the Italian way of seeing the world. Whether you've already learned some Italian or you're curious about it, this book will help you go deeper. You'll get to know the language the way it's really spoken by local people, through stories, gestures, habits, and moments. Every phrase in this book brings you one step closer to understanding a unique way of life. So, as the Italians would say, *Iniziamo!* ("Let's get started!")

1 Historical, Cultural, and Linguistic Context

Before exploring the words and expressions that give Italian its beauty, it is important to understand where the language comes from and how it evolved into one of the most loved languages in the world. This chapter traces the journey of Italian, from its roots in Latin and its ties to regional dialects, to its role in art, music, and literature. It also follows Italian beyond the borders of Italy, showing how it became a language spoken by many in communities around the world. By the end of this chapter, you will see how every phrase in this book carries a story shaped by centuries of culture, creativity, and human connection.

Latin Roots

The story of Italian begins long before Italy existed as a nation. Its origins lie in Latin, specifically, the Latin spoken by ordinary people during the height of the Roman Empire. The Latin used by scholars and poets (known as Classical Latin) was formal, structured, and refined, while the Latin spoken by soldiers, merchants, and farmers was more flexible and spontaneous. This spoken form, known as Vulgar Latin, from *vulgus*, meaning "common people," was the language of daily life, of marketplaces and military camps, of family stories and laughter. It was a living language, changing with every generation and across every province within the empire. Unlike the Classical Latin of those such as scholar Cicero and poet Virgil, which followed strict grammatical rules, Vulgar Latin evolved constantly. People shortened words, softened sounds, and simplified endings to make conversation easier. Over generations, these small variations transformed the language; for example, *panem* became *pane* in Italian (in English, "bread") and *aquam* became *acqua*, meaning "water."

The Birth of the Romance Languages

From these modest shifts of Vulgar Latin grew the rich family of Romance languages, including Italian, Spanish, Portuguese, and French. As the Roman Empire expanded, Vulgar Latin traveled with soldiers, settlers, and traders, adapting to the sounds of local languages. It mingled with Celtic in Gaul, with Iberian in Spain, and with Greek in southern Italy. Language, like culture, was never still. When Latin met other languages, it absorbed new words and lost others, creating variations that reflected local life. The Latin of the Alps was not the Latin of Sicily, and the Latin of the African coast also sounded different.

When the Roman Empire fell in the fifth century, roads broke down, trade declined, and communication between provinces weakened. Without a central power to keep the language uniform, Latin splintered. Over time, these regional varieties developed into the distinct Romance languages, each preserving traces of their ancestors but also with their own rhythm. On the Italian peninsula, during the time following the empire's fall, language change evolved slowly and unevenly. Northern Italy absorbed influences from Germanic tribes and later from French, leaving behind sharp consonants. Southern Italy, meanwhile, retained a soft cadence and a rich vocabulary after the centuries of Greek and Arabic it had been exposed to.

Florence and the Birth of Literary Italian

Among the many dialects that emerged in the centuries following the fall of the Roman Empire, the Tuscan dialect stood out for its musicality and precision. Its vowel endings gave it a natural harmony, while its consonants glided smoothly from one to another. For example, the Tuscan habit of pronouncing the letter *c* softly, as in *cena* (in English, "dinner"), or the characteristic *g* sound in *giorno*, meaning "day," gave the language a musical elegance that captivated listeners.

It was in the Tuscan city of Florence that Italy's literary giants shaped the foundation of the Italian language as a literary and later national standard beloved today. The city's wealth nurtured a spirit of creativity and intellectual freedom, allowing figures like Dante Alighieri, Francesco Petrarca (Petrarch), and Giovanni Boccaccio to write masterpieces that transformed Italian. Dante's epic poem, *Divine Comedy* (first printed in 1472), for example, was revolutionary because it used the speech of ordinary Florentines instead of Latin, which had long been utilized by scholars and the Church. His work showed that the everyday language of the Florentines could convey the same depth of thought and emotion found in the philosophical and theological works traditionally written in Latin. Petrarch refined the Florentine dialect concurrently with Dante, transforming it into a means of reflection in his *Canzoniere* (first printed in 1470), a collection of sonnets that explore love and the passage of time. During the same period, Boccaccio expanded the vernacular in *The Decameron* (circulated in manuscript form in the 1370s, and first printed in 1470), a collection of short stories that uses vivid dialogue and storytelling to portray the desires and flaws of people from all walks of life. Together, these authors gave the Florentine dialect both intellectual prestige and emotional range, turning it from a simple dialect into the foundation of modern Italian.

The Italian Renaissance

As artists, scholars, and scientists continued to gather in the thriving city during this time, the language flourished. Italy was entering a new time of creativity and discovery: the Italian Renaissance, a cultural movement that occurred in Florence between the fourteenth century and sixteenth century, and revived the art, literature, and learning of classical Greece and Rome. Fueled by wealthy families such as the Medici, the city became a center for artists, humanists, and scientists whose work reshaped Europe. Leonardo da Vinci was filling his notebooks in Florentine as he explored anatomy, light, and mechanics. Meanwhile, Galileo Galilei chose Latin and also Florentine for his scientific works. In workshops and studios, Florentine became the language of innovation. Painters discussed perspective and proportion in Florentine; musicians composed in it; architects designed through it. It was a language capable of expressing both mathematical precision and emotional intensity. By the sixteenth century, scholars like Pietro Bembo codified Florentine Tuscan as the model for proper Italian, emphasizing its balance and clarity.

Opera was born at the edge of the Italian Renaissance. Created in Florence around the turn of the seventeenth century, it blended poetry, music, and theater into a single art form. And the Italian language, with its pure vowels and melodic phrasing, proved the perfect vehicle for this new style of storytelling. As opera spread through Europe, Italian became the universal language of music. To this day, performers around the world use Italian words to describe tempo and feeling: *allegro* for "lively," *adagio* for "slowly," *forte* for "strong," and *piano* for "soft." These terms, still written in scores everywhere, testify to Italy and Italian's influence. In fact, the Italian of the Renaissance still feels close to that spoken today. Words like *amore*, "love" in English; *casa*, which translates to "house"; and *mare*, which means "sea," have changed little. Language, in Italy, is a bridge between past and present, between spoken sound and cultural memory.

Italian Dialects

Beyond the Florentine Tuscan dialect of Florence, there is a whole breadth of different Italian dialects to explore. These dialects are not just different accents; they are languages that evolved from Latin in different directions. And each has much to offer in understanding not just Italian vocabulary but the history and culture of this beloved country. In addition to Florentine, the following are common dialects of the Italian language:

- Venetian (in the northern region of Veneto, including Venice)
- Lombard (in the northern region of Lombardy, including Milan; and in parts of eastern Piedmont and the western part of the Trentino region)
- Piedmontese (in the northern region of Piedmont, including Turin)
- Emilian-Romagnol (in the northern region of Emilia-Romagna, including Bologna and Parma)
- Neapolitan (in the southern region of Campania, including Naples, and in southern Italy)
- Sicilian (in the island of Sicily and in southern Italy)
- Sardinian (in the island of Sardinia)

Venetian reflects centuries of trade across the Adriatic, showing contact with Germanic and Slavic peoples. Lombard and Piedmontese, shaped by northern Europe and proximity to France and Switzerland, carry Gallo-Italic features distinct from central Italian speech. Emilian-Romagnol bridges northern and central Italy, blending influences from both regions. Neapolitan developed in the vibrant cultural crossroads of southern Italy, absorbing elements from Spanish rule and earlier Mediterranean exchanges. Sicilian carries deep traces of Arabic, Greek, and Spanish presence, while Sardinian, long isolated from the mainland, preserves Latin features that disappeared elsewhere.

When Italy became one country in 1861, only a small minority spoke standard Italian, that is, the Florentine dialect.

Most people communicated in dialects within their towns and families, as the country previously consisted of separate city-states and kingdoms. Following unification, the new government promoted education to spread the national language, but the change was gradual. It was radio and TV in the twentieth century that finally made Italian accessible to all (more on this later). Yet dialects never quite disappeared, and even today, dialects shape identity. In Naples, *guaglione* means "boy," while it is *ragazzo* in standard Italian. In Venice, *schiao*, once meaning "I am your slave," became *ciao*, a friendly greeting now known around the world. In Sicily, *bedda* (*bella* in standard Italian) means "beautiful." In Rome, the exclamation *aho!* can convey surprise, affection, or mild irritation depending on tone. Dialects color everyday Italian; many expressions in standard speech have dialect origins. Even Italians who no longer speak a certain dialect fluently may use a word or two from their grandparents, a reminder of their roots.

Music, cinema, and popular culture also keep dialects alive. The soulful songs of Naples, from "O sole mio" to "Funiculì Funiculà," have carried local language across the globe. Singers like Pino Daniele and Fabrizio De André blended Italian and dialect to create music that's accessible yet deeply regional. Modern films and comedies continue this tradition, with each accent and each phrase carrying a sense of place and belonging. Italy's linguistic diversity is not a barrier but a reflection of its vitality.

Beyond Italy

The journey of the Italian language did not stop at Italy's or even Europe's borders. Between the late nineteenth and early twentieth centuries, millions of Italians left their homeland in search of opportunity. They carried with them recipes, songs, and the rhythms of their speech. In New York, Boston, Buenos Aires, São Paulo, and Melbourne, Italian neighborhoods bloomed. The sounds of the Italian language mixed with English, Spanish, and Portuguese, creating new forms of expression. Italian words entered other languages; *pizza*, *pasta*, *bravo*, *opera*, became part of a shared global vocabulary.

Italian remains an emotional link for millions of descendants abroad. For Italian Americans, Argentine Italians, and others, speaking even a few words connects them to ancestry and belonging, and across generations, language becomes memory. Today, Italian is an official language not only in Italy, but also Switzerland, San Marino, and the Vatican, and is one of the European Union's official languages. It is studied in schools and universities around the world. Its appeal lies not only in its heritage but in its sound and the way it flows like music. In the twenty-first century, Italian stands at a crossroads between tradition and innovation.

Technology, Inclusion, and the Future of Italian

Technology has introduced new words and new rhythms to the Italian language. From radio to the Internet, ever-evolving digital conversations blend Italian and English: for example, *un* selfie *perfetto, lo* streaming *del concerto, scrollare le notizie.* Podcasts, YouTube channels, and social media pages also bring Italian voices to new generations of learners and admirers. Young people create slang, and playful adaptations show a language that grows while keeping its own melody.

There is also a movement toward inclusivity and balance. Because Italian grammar is gendered, speakers today discuss how to make it more representative of modern society. Some experiment with symbols like the schwa (ə) to neutralize gender endings; others emphasize equality through new expressions and awareness. These conversations reveal that Italian is alive, listening, adjusting, responding to its time.

The language also continues to thrive and evolve through art and media. Italian cinema, from Fellini to Sorrentino, carries the rhythm of its speech across cultures. Meanwhile, Italian pop music blends dialects and slang, creating a living dictionary of change.

But despite globalization, Italian retains its distinct personality. To speak Italian is to slow down, to savor sound and meaning. Italians often say *vivere alla giornata*, that is, "to live day by day." This phrase captures the nation's approach to life: mindful, expressive, and unhurried. In a world driven by efficiency, Italian reminds people of connection. It celebrates community over isolation, pleasure over hurry, and art over practicality. Through its expressions, you can glimpse a philosophy rooted in appreciation: finding joy in beauty and strength in belonging.

Continuing Your Journey Through Italian

This book continues that invitation to connect and savor life. As you explore the words and expressions ahead, you will discover that every phrase opens a window into the Italian soul. You will see how a greeting conveys friendship, how a culinary term expresses philosophy, and how an idiom captures humor.

Additionally, each phrase you speak continues a story that began long ago and still evolves today. Italian lives in gestures, in laughter, in the music of its syllables. As you learn and practice this language, you become part of a living chain that links the ancient world to the modern one. To speak Italian, even a little, is to share in its charm, passion, and poetry, to live, if only for a moment, *all'italiana*, the Italian way.

Italian Pronunciation and Grammar Guide

Learning Italian starts with pronunciation and grammar. This chapter offers a practical introduction to these foundational building blocks, to help you speak and understand the language. To make pronunciation easier to understand, the explanations that follow are based on English sounds. Although this may simplify some details, it will give you a solid base for sounding natural and being understood when you speak Italian. As you read this chapter, you will discover how letters are pronounced, how stress and rhythm shape the flow of Italian, and how sentences come together to form meaning. You will explore nouns, articles, verbs, and basic sentence patterns so that each word in the following chapters comes alive when you read and say it aloud.

The Alphabet

The Italian alphabet has twenty-one letters. It does not include *j*, *k*, *w*, *x*, or *y*, though you may see them in foreign words or names. The vowels (*a*, *e*, *i*, *o*, *u*) are pure sounds and form the heart of Italian pronunciation. The Italian vowel *a* sounds like *ah* in "father." The vowel *e* can be open, like *e* in "wet," or closed, like *ai* in "fair." The vowel *i* sounds like *ee* in "see," while the vowel *o* can be open, like *o* in "off," or closed, like *oh* in "note." The vowel *u* sounds like *oo* in "moon." These seven vowel sounds give Italian its clear and consistent quality.

Consonants are generally pronounced as written. However, the letters *c* and *g* can change sound depending on what follows them:

ce, ci	***ch*** **("church")**	**e.g.,** ***cena, cibo***
ca, co, cu, ch	***k*** **("car")**	**e.g.,** ***casa, cono, cubo, chiesa***
ge, gi	***j*** **("jam")**	**e.g.,** ***gente, giro***
ga, go, gu, gh	***g*** **("go")**	**e.g.,** ***gala, gola, gusto, ghiro***

Double consonants, such as *pp*, *tt*, or *mm*, are held longer and produce a longer sound compared to single ones. For example, *Papa* means "Pope," while *pappa* means "baby food."

As far as stress, it usually falls on the second-to-last syllable. For example, *PApa*. However, exceptions exist and are often marked with an accent, as in *perCHÉ* ("why" or "because," with the same pronunciation).

Listening to native speakers, as well as repeating what is said, is the best way to capture the stress of words and rhythm. When reading aloud, open your mouth fully, pronounce every letter, and let the sound travel.

Word Number and Gender

Every Italian noun has both a number (that is, singular or plural) and a gender, either masculine or feminine. The number and gender affect the form of other words in the sentence. Most masculine nouns form the plural by changing the final -*o* to -*i* (*vaso* becomes *vasi*, from "vase" to "vases"), and most feminine nouns change the final -*a* to -*e* (*casa* becomes *case*, from "house" to "houses"), though some singular nouns also end in -*e* (*carne*, meaning "meat") and can be masculine or feminine, so it's best to memorize their gender.

Adjectives agree with the nouns they describe in both gender (masculine or feminine) and number (singular or plural). The phrase *un ragazzo alto* means "a tall boy," and *una ragazza alta* means "a tall girl." The adjective changes from -*o* to -*a* to match the gender of the singular noun. When plural, *ragazzi alti* means "tall boys," and *ragazze alte* means "tall girls." This harmony between nouns and adjectives is one reason Italian sounds balanced.

Verbs

Just as vowels are at the heart of Italian pronunciation, verbs are at the heart of Italian grammar. The most essential verb is *essere* ("to be"), used to describe identity, state, or condition:

io sono ("I am")	*tu sei* ("you are")	*lui/lei è* ("he/she is")	*noi siamo* ("we are")	*voi siete* ("you are"; plural)	*loro sono* ("they are")

Another key verb is *avere* ("to have"):

io ho ("I have")	*tu hai* ("you have")	*lui/lei ha* ("he/she has")	*noi abbiamo* ("we have")	*voi avete* ("you have"; plural)	*loro hanno* ("they have")

Together, *essere* and *avere* form the foundation for many other tenses.

Other important verbs include *fare* ("to do, to make"), *andare* ("to go"), and *volere* ("to want"):

io faccio ("I do, make")	*tu fai* ("you do, make")	*lui/lei fa* ("he/she does, makes")	*noi facciamo* ("we do, make")	*voi fate* ("you do, make"; plural)	*loro fanno* ("they do, make")
io vado ("I go")	*tu vai* ("you go")	*lui/lei va* ("he/she goes")	*noi andiamo* ("we go")	*voi andate* ("you go"; plural)	*loro vanno* ("they go")
io voglio ("I want")	*tu vuoi* ("you want")	*lui/lei vuole* ("he/she wants")	*noi vogliamo* ("we want")	*voi volete* ("you want"; plural)	*loro vogliono* ("they want")

Italian verbs change their endings to match the subject. Because the verb ending reveals the subject, Italian often omits the subject pronoun (for example, instead of saying *noi siamo*, you can simply say *siamo*, meaning "we are").

Italian sentences also generally follow subject-verb-object order, as in *Io mangio la pizza* ("I eat pizza"), but again, you can simply say *Mangio la pizza* without the *io*, and the meaning remains clear.

Negation is simple, just place the Italian word *non* before the verb. For instance, *Io non parlo italiano* means "I do not speak Italian."

Questions can be asked just by changing tone and rising intonation at the end of the question. For example: *Tu parli italiano?* ("Do you speak Italian?").

Prepositions link ideas and locations. The Italian preposition *a* means "to" or "in" when talking about being in a city (*a Roma*); the preposition *in* is used for countries (*in Italia*). *Di* is for possession (*Questo è il libro di Marco*: "This is Marco's book"). *Con* means "with" (*Esco con Matteo*: "I go out with Matteo"). Though small, these words carry much meaning and appear constantly in Italian sentences.

Speaking the Words Out Loud

When pronunciation, grammar, words, and rhythm come together, Italian starts to flow naturally. Begin by saying simple words from this book out loud. Speaking often helps you internalize not only the words themselves but also the melody and rhythm of the language. Italian grammar may look detailed at first, but it follows clear and consistent patterns, with some irregularities. Once you understand the basics, you can build your own sentences and express original ideas. The goal isn't to sound perfect, it's to speak freely and let the language come alive in your voice.

3

Greetings, Farewells, and Conversations

In Italian, everyday conversations are full of short yet powerful words and expressions that carry far more meaning than their literal translations. Greetings like *ciao* and *piacere* or farewells such as *addio* and *buonanotte* are not just polite remarks, but ways of building connection. Words like *uffa* capture frustration in a single sound, while phrases such as *ti voglio bene* convey deep affection and care without needing many words. In this chapter, you will explore these different greetings, farewells, and other expressions of communication. Learning these will help you go beyond grammar and vocabulary, allowing you to feel immersed in the rhythm of Italian life, whether you are traveling in the country or enjoying the language at home.

Accidenti INTERJECTION

(ahc-chee-DEHN-tee)

Darn; No way; Wow

This common Italian exclamation, used to express surprise, frustration, or mild annoyance, is equivalent to English expressions like "darn," "no way," or "wow." ***Accidenti*** is used when something unexpected or irritating happens. For example, if you spill espresso on your shirt or miss a train, you might say, "***Accidenti!***" as an expression of frustration or surprise. The word ***accidenti*** derives from the verb *accadere* meaning "to happen" or "to occur" and was first used to wish misfortune upon someone. Over time, it became a versatile and casual exclamation for everyday speech; it's never as strong as cursing or a more serious expression of annoyance. In Italian culture, ***accidenti*** is widely used in informal spoken contexts. While the word may have originated with more serious connotations, today it's more of a lighthearted or even humorous interjection, helping to convey a range of emotions from mild irritation to surprise. For example, to express surprise, you might say, "***Accidenti!*** *Che bella notizia!*" which translates to "No way! That's wonderful news!"

Similar Words, Different Meanings The word ***accidenti*** should not be confused with the word *accidente*, a noun used to talk about an unexpected or negative event that usually causes harm or damage. It is also different from the word *incidente*, a noun used to indicate a serious accident or wreck.

Addio INTERJECTION

(ahd-DEE-oh)

Goodbye forever

Addio is more than just the Italian word for "goodbye." Unlike the casual *ciao* when ending a phone call or the formal *arrivederci* when leaving a dinner party, ***addio*** is reserved for moments that feel final and deeply emotional. It's a farewell used when the future is uncertain or when the parting may be permanent. It carries the weight of something profound. The word itself comes from the Latin expression *ad Deum*, meaning "to God." This origin gives it a serious, almost spiritual feeling, as if the speaker is saying to the other person that they are in God's care. Historically, ***addio*** was often used in situations where departure meant great distance or danger, such as leaving for war, going to faraway lands, or heading off on a journey with little chance of return. Today, ***addio*** continues to carry that same gravity. It is not part of everyday language but rather reserved for life-changing occasions. A loved one moving abroad, the close of an important life chapter, or the final goodbye to someone dear, are all moments that might call for the word ***addio***. It remains one of the simplest yet moving expressions in the Italian language.

Allora ADVERB, INTERJECTION

(ahl-LOH-rah)

Well; So then

Allora is one of those untranslatable words that holds a special place in the Italian language. It's a word you'll hear constantly in everyday conversation, used to fill pauses, change topic, or introduce a new thought. ***Allora*** doesn't translate perfectly into English, but its closest equivalents might be "well" or "so then," depending on context. The magic of ***allora*** lies in its versatility. It's a word that can help start a sentence, clarify something, or signal a change in tone. Imagine an Italian conversation where the speaker pauses to gather their thoughts; ***allora*** often comes in as a cue, a kind of short pause, meaning "well" before continuing. This word is also used to signal a conclusion or a transition, like saying "so then" in English when moving from one topic to another. But it can also express surprise, impatience, or emphasis, depending on how it's said. In some ways, ***allora*** embodies the relaxed nature of Italian conversation: a way of drawing things together while giving space for the interaction to continue. The word's origins trace back to *ad illam hōram* in Latin, meaning "at that time," which emphasizes its connection to moments and transitions. Today, it remains a very common conversational tool that helps bridge thoughts, make statements less abrupt, and encourage the flow of conversation. Using ***allora*** is an instant way to connect with locals and embrace the conversational pace of Italy.

Auguri INTERJECTION, NOUN

(ow-GOO-ree)

Best wishes; Congratulations

Auguri is a word filled with warmth and good intentions. In Italian, it's commonly used to wish someone happiness, success, or good fortune, just like saying "best wishes" or "congratulations" in English. At a birthday party, a wedding, or during a holiday, you'll hear Italians exclaiming "***Auguri!***" as a way of celebrating and wishing well for someone. The strength of this word lies in its versatility. You can use it in both formal or informal contexts, and it always conveys a sense of kindness and good cheer. When you wish someone ***auguri*** on their special day, it's not just a customary phrase but an expression of real joy for their happiness. This word comes from the Latin *augurium*, which referred to favorable signs, further emphasizing its association with good fortune. In its essence, ***auguri*** celebrates the moments that matter, such as birthdays, weddings, and other milestones. Simply saying "***Auguri!***" when someone shares news or a life event is a great way to show warmth and appreciation. It's a simple yet powerful word that encapsulates the spirit of Italian togetherness and celebration.

Sending You Birthday Wishes You might hear the adjective *tanti* before the word ***auguri***, that is, *tanti* ***auguri***. This literally means "many wishes" and makes the expression even warmer and more affectionate. It's the phrase most often used in birthday greetings: *Tanti* ***auguri*** *di buon compleanno!* means "Many wishes for a happy birthday!"

Baci e abbracci PHRASE

(BAH-chee eh ahb-BRAH-cchee)

Hugs and kisses

Baci e abbracci is a classic Italian expression of affection that literally means "kisses and hugs." It's commonly used at the end of letters, emails, or messages to convey a sense of closeness. Much like "hugs and kisses" in English, it creates an affectionate closing that feels personal and warm. The word *baci* comes from *bacio* ("kiss"), while *abbracci* comes from *abbraccio* ("hug"). When combined in the plural form, they form a powerful expression that communicates bonds of friendship, love, or family ties. This phrase is used in informal contexts, among people who know each other well. You might end a note to a friend with, "*A presto, **baci e abbracci**!*" (in English, "See you soon, hugs and kisses!"). Parents often use it when writing to children, friends include it in casual correspondence, and partners may choose it as a playful sign-off. It is rarely, if ever, used in formal writing, where more neutral closings such as *Cordiali saluti* or *Distinti saluti* ("Kind regards") are preferred. ***Baci e abbracci*** does not have to be romantic; it can just express affection and care. The phrase reflects the Italian cultural emphasis on open displays of emotion and valuing close personal relationships. The origin lies in everyday Italian customs: Kissing on the cheeks and hugging are traditional greetings and farewells among family and friends.

Basta INTERJECTION

(BAH-stah)

Enough; Stop

Basta is the informal Italian word for "enough," and it's used to signal that something should stop immediately. It's what you use when something needs to end, like an annoying situation, a conversation that's dragging, or someone going too far. For example: ***Basta** parlare, andiamo!* (in English, "Enough talking, let's go!"). It's a short, powerful word that carries a lot of weight, making it an essential part of Italian daily expression. You might hear it in a heated discussion, as a parent tells their child to stop misbehaving, or in a conversation when someone feels they have had enough of a particular topic. ***Basta*** is a direct word; there's no need for elaborate explanations. For those who travel to Italy, knowing the meaning of the word ***basta*** can be important for recognizing when to back off in social situations, or when an Italian is trying to indicate that the current behavior, conversation, or action is no longer acceptable. ***Basta*** carries a history of its own, stemming from the Latin *bastāre*, meaning "to endure." Even though ***basta*** is short, it carries a strong sense of finality. It shows the importance of setting limits and making those limits clear to others with just one simple word.

Bentornato | Bentornata

INTERJECTION, ADJECTIVE

(behn-tor-NAH-toh) | (behn-tor-NAH-tah)

Welcome back

Bentornato is the warm and friendly Italian way of saying "welcome back." It's a greeting that conveys joy and appreciation and it is usually used when someone returns after being away for a while. The word ***bentornato*** comes from the combination of *ben* ("well") and *tornato* ("returned"), literally meaning "well returned," which reflects the warmth of the welcome. In Italy, this greeting is often used not just for people who have been gone for an extended period, but also when returning to familiar spaces or situations. For example, you might hear "***Bentornato!***" when you walk back into your favorite café after a few days away. It has a sense of community and belonging attached to it, reflecting the Italian appreciation for connection. You'll often hear it from friends, family, or colleagues, particularly in close-knit communities. As a tourist, if someone says "***Bentornato***" to you, it can be a sign that you have made a positive impression and are now part of the social fabric. It's a reaffirmation that you've been missed and are welcomed back with open arms, and it's also a beautiful reminder of how Italians value presence. ***Bentornato*** is traditionally used when addressing a male, while ***bentornata*** is traditionally used when addressing a female. In the plural form, when addressing a group of males or those of mixed gender, *bentornati* is used; *bentornate* is for a group of females.

Benvenuto | Benvenuta

INTERJECTION, ADJECTIVE

(ben-veh-NOO-toh) | (ben-veh-NOO-tah)

Welcome

If *bentornato* means "welcome back," then ***benvenuto*** is the classic Italian way of saying "welcome" to someone arriving for the first time. It's the greeting you'll hear when meeting someone new, when a guest arrives at your home, or when you want to express appreciation for someone's presence. The word itself combines *ben* ("well") and *venuto* ("came," from the Italian verb *venire*), literally meaning "well came." Like many Italian expressions, the ending is traditionally changed to match the gender of the person being addressed: ***benvenuto*** for a male, ***benvenuta*** for a female. If addressing a group of people, *benvenuti* is used for mixed groups or all males, while *benvenute* is used when the group is entirely female. You might hear ***benvenuto*** when arriving at someone's house; for example: ***Benvenuto*** *a casa nostra!* is "Welcome to our home!" There is also another less common variation, *benarrivato* (or *benarrivata* in the feminine form), which literally means "well arrived." *Benarrivato* is often heard in more formal settings, for example when welcoming people after a journey or a trip. Italians value these greetings because they carry a sense of hospitality. The ***benvenuto*** and ***benvenuta*** expressions reflect the cultural importance of making people feel included and appreciated.

Bravo | Brava ADJECTIVE, INTERJECTION

(BRAH-voh) | (BRAH-vah)

Good; Good job

The word ***bravo*** is one of the most common and recognizable expressions of praise in Italy. It's used as an adjective and also to congratulate someone on a job well done, whether they have just performed in a play, completed a project, or cooked a great meal. The word ***bravo*** comes from the Latin *pravus*, meaning "crooked" or "depraved." In modern Italian, however, its meaning has shifted to express admiration and approval. You'll hear ***bravo*** frequently in Italy, especially in informal and everyday settings. It's not reserved only for major achievements; it can be used to celebrate small successes too. For example, after a child completes their homework, a parent might say, "***Bravo!***" to acknowledge their effort. Similarly, at work, a colleague might say, "***Bravo** per la presentazione!*" meaning "Well done on the presentation!" It's a simple yet sincere way of showing appreciation. In addition, ***bravo*** can act as a form of encouragement. After a concert or performance, shouting "***Bravo!***" from the audience is one of the most traditional ways to recognize the artist's talent. Because ***bravo*** is also an adjective, it changes its form depending on gender and number. Traditionally, for a female, you would say ***brava***; for more than one male or a mixed group, *bravi*; and for a group of females, *brave*. For example: ***Brava** Maria!* or *Bravi bambini!* ("Well done, children!").

Buon viaggio **PHRASE**

(bwohn vee-AH-jjoh)

Safe travels; Have a good trip

Buon viaggio is a common Italian expression used to wish someone a pleasant and safe journey. The phrase is composed of two words: *buon*, which means "good," and *viaggio*, which means "journey" or "trip." Together, ***buon viaggio*** literally translates to "good trip" or, better, "have a good trip." In Italian culture, saying ***buon viaggio*** is a way of expressing care and affection toward someone who is about to travel. It's a traditional and thoughtful way of wishing someone well as they leave, whether they are going on a short vacation or international adventure, or relocating to a new place. This phrase is often heard when family members, friends, or colleagues are saying goodbye at airports, train stations, or even just at the doorstep. It's a warm phrase that reflects Italy's deep-rooted emphasis on relationships and meaningful communication. Travelers may also hear ***buon viaggio*** from locals when they're about to depart, especially in more personal or friendly settings. Whether spoken in a casual tone or as part of a farewell, ***buon viaggio*** is always a kind and encouraging message. So, next time someone you know is heading off on a journey, you might consider borrowing from the Italians and saying "***Buon viaggio!***"

Buonanotte INTERJECTION

(bwoh-nah-NOHT-teh)

Good night

In Italy, ***buonanotte*** is a common phrase used to wish someone a peaceful and restful night. It can be written either as a single word: ***buonanotte***, or as two separate words, *buona notte*. This simple expression is the Italian equivalent of "good night," and it carries affection and care. The phrase is formed of *buona*, the feminine singular adjective meaning "good," and *notte*, meaning "night." Together, they directly translate to "good night." While the meaning is straightforward, the cultural aspect of the phrase is what makes it special. ***Buonanotte*** is often said to loved ones before going to bed or when leaving an evening gathering, and it serves as both a farewell and a blessing for rest. All across Italy, families often exchange a warm ***buonanotte*** each evening, making it a part of their nightly routine. Parents often say it to their children, sometimes adding the phrase *sogni d'oro*, literally "golden dreams," which better translates to the English "sweet dreams." This affectionate phrase enhances the warmth of the good night wish. Used among friends, family, and partners, ***buonanotte*** reflects the Italian emphasis on connection and care. It is a way of wishing peace, serenity, and sweet rest at the close of the day.

Word Origins **The Italian word *notte* comes from the Latin *nox*, meaning "night." This root word persisted as Latin evolved into Italian, which is why you still see it in related words like *notturno* ("nighttime") and *notte fonda* ("late night").**

Buongiorno INTERJECTION

(bwohn-JOR-noh)

Good morning

Buongiorno has deep roots in Italian culture as one of the most common ways to greet people in the morning. The word itself is a compound of the masculine and singular adjective *buon* ("good"), and the masculine noun *giorno* ("day"), directly translating to "good day." However, the correct translation in English is "good morning" as this greeting is mostly used between 5 a.m. and 12 p.m. Just like the greetings *buonasera*, meaning "good evening," and *buonanotte*, meaning "good night," ***buongiorno*** can be written as one single word (more common today) or as two separate words: *buon giorno* (less common today). An alternative of this greeting used in certain regions is *buondì*, which also means "good morning." In this case, the adjective *buon* is accompanied by the Italian noun *dì*, which is a formal and literary form of the word *giorno* ("day"). The greeting ***buongiorno*** can be used in both formal and informal situations. For example, you might say, "***Buongiorno****, professore*" to a professor, or simply "***Buongiorno***" to a friend when you meet them in the morning.

Pronunciation Matters The pronunciation here is important. When saying ***buongiorno***, make sure to pronounce both vowels *u* and *o*. Also, the consonant *g* should be pronounced softly, like the *g* sound in "journey," not like the hard *g* in "go." Practicing it out loud will help you sound more natural.

Che bello PHRASE

(keh BEHL-loh)

How beautiful; How nice

The expression ***che bello*** is one of the most popular informal phrases in Italian, used to show admiration and excitement. While the literal translation is "how beautiful" or "how nice," the phrase is not limited to physical beauty. Instead, it conveys a broader sense of joy and appreciation. For example, when walking through the streets of Rome and seeing the Colosseum, you might exclaim, "***Che bello!***" to capture your awe. Similarly, if a friend tells you they are heading to Florence for a summer vacation, responding with "***Che bello!***" (which can translate to "How nice!") shows your excitement and happiness for them. You might also hear ***che bello*** in everyday life when someone shares good news, like getting a promotion or buying a house. From a grammar perspective, *che* means "what," and *bello* is the singular masculine form of the adjective meaning "beautiful" or "nice." The Italian word *bello* comes from the Latin adjective *bellus*, a diminutive of the Latin *bonus*, which originally meant "handsome," "charming," or "pleasant." In modern Italian, the word has broadened beyond physical beauty to also express admiration, enjoyment, and positivity, which is why ***che bello*** can be translated as "how beautiful," "how nice," or even "how cool," depending on the context.

Che fortuna! EXCLAMATION

(keh for-TOO-nah)

How lucky!; What luck!

Che fortuna! is a very common Italian exclamation used to react to a positive event that happens unexpectedly or through chance. Literally meaning "What luck!" this Italian expression is used in everyday conversation to acknowledge moments when things go well. In daily life, ***Che fortuna!*** can refer to both small and significant events. Finding a parking spot in a crowded city, catching a train just before it leaves, or discovering that a school test has been postponed are all situations where an Italian speaker might instinctively say "***Che fortuna!***" The phrase helps frame the event as something favorable granted by circumstance rather than control. Grammatically, the expression follows a common Italian exclamatory structure using *che* ("what") followed by a noun. This same structure appears in phrases such as *che peccato* ("what a shame") or *che sorpresa* ("what a surprise"). The Italian phrase is fixed and does not change form, which makes it easy for you to reuse. When ***Che fortuna!*** is said enthusiastically, it expresses genuine happiness or relief; when said with irony, it can take on a sarcastic meaning, implying that the situation is not fortunate at all. Context and intonation determine whether the phrase is sincere or ironic. For language learners, ***Che fortuna!*** is a useful and natural expression that fits easily into conversation. It allows speakers to react quickly without needing a full sentence.

Ci sto VERB, PHRASE

(chee STOH)

I'm in; I'm game

Ci sto is a colloquial Italian phrase that reflects the country's emphasis on spontaneity and social engagement. The literal translation of ***ci sto*** is "there (I) stay," with *ci* meaning "there" and *sto* coming from the verb *stare* (in English, "to stay"). The expression is better understood as "I'm in" or "I'm game," which conveys enthusiasm and readiness to join in on an activity or plan. In Italy, where social gatherings and spontaneous plans are central to the culture, ***ci sto*** is often used to show agreement. Whether a friend invites you for an impromptu coffee or someone suggests a road trip, ***ci sto*** is the perfect response to show you're excited and willing to participate. It reflects the Italian attitude of living in the moment and making the most of life's unplanned opportunities. The plural form of ***ci sto*** is *ci stiamo*, which translates to "we're in" or "we're game." This is commonly used when a group of people agrees to participate in an activity together. For example, if a group of friends is discussing plans, someone might say, "*Ci stiamo*," signaling that the whole group is ready to join in. Both ***ci sto*** and *ci stiamo* capture the Italian love for connection, spontaneity, and shared enjoyment.

I'm *Not* In The negative version of ***ci sto***, *non* ***ci sto***, means "I'm not okay with that" or "I won't go along with it." It's used to refuse an idea, rule, or situation, and often to set a boundary: *A queste condizioni non* ***ci sto*** ("Under these conditions I'm not in").

Ci vediamo VERB, PHRASE

(chee veh-DYAH-moh)

See you; We'll see each other

Ci vediamo is a common Italian way to say goodbye, with the expectation of seeing the person again soon. It literally translates to "(we) ourselves see," and it stems from the verb *vedersi*, which means "to see each other." ***Ci vediamo*** uses the plural reflexive pronoun (also called a reciprocal pronoun) *ci*, meaning "ourselves," which means that the action (seeing) is shared between two or more people. This grammatical structure reflects the emphasis in Italian on mutual actions and social connection. In the case of ***ci vediamo***, the verb is in the present tense, first-person plural *noi* ("we"), but the phrase can be adapted to different tenses and pronouns depending on the situation. For example, *ci vedremo* (translating to "we will see each other") uses the future tense to suggest a meeting that is less immediate or less certain, perhaps still to be arranged. ***Ci vediamo*** implies something already planned or imminent. In everyday conversation, ***ci vediamo*** is used informally to indicate that you will see the person again, often in the near future. You would use it when leaving a gathering, a café, or after an outing with friends. For instance, after a lunch with a friend, you might say, "***Ci vediamo*** *domani*" (in English, "We'll see each other tomorrow," or "See you tomorrow").

Ciao INTERJECTION

(chow)

Hello; Bye

Ciao is one of the most recognizable Italian words, used around the world as both a greeting and a farewell. It works equally well when saying "hello" and when saying "bye" in informal situations, best suited for friends, family, and people you already know rather than for professional or formal contexts. The word ***ciao*** comes from the Venetian word *schiao*, which literally meant "I am your slave" or "at your service." In seventeenth-century Venice, this was an expression of respect and humility, similar to saying "yours truly." Over time, however, the phrase lost its original formality and evolved into the much shorter and friendlier ***ciao***. The initial *s* was dropped, and the word was adopted across Italy as a casual greeting or way to say goodbye. Today, ***ciao*** is deeply ingrained in Italian daily life. You might say "***Ciao***" when arriving at a friend's house, entering a classroom, or leaving dinner with family. Whether it is being used to say hi or bye depends on the context. For example, ***Ciao**, come stai?* means "Hi, how are you?" while ***Ciao**, a domani!* means "Bye, see you tomorrow!" Beyond Italy, ***ciao*** is often heard in countries like France, Spain, and even English-speaking places. Still, Italians generally reserve it for informal situations, using more formal greetings like *buongiorno* or *arrivederci* in professional settings.

Come stai? PHRASE

(KOH-meh STAH-ee)

How are you?

Come stai? is one of the most essential phrases in Italian and is used to ask someone how they are doing. While the literal translation is "How do you stay?" the English equivalent is "How are you?" This phrase is informal, often used among friends, family, or people you already know. In contrast, in professional or formal contexts, you would use *Come sta?*, where the verb *stare* changes from the informal second-person singular *tu* (*stai*) to the formal *Lei (sta)*. *Lei* is the same word as the third-person pronoun meaning "she," but, when capitalized, serves as the formal form of "you" in Italian. This dual role of *Lei* is explained further under *Dammi del tu*. Asking ***Come stai?*** or *Come sta?* is a genuine way of showing care and interest in someone's well-being, and the reply is often expected to be more than just *bene* ("well"). Italians usually elaborate, adding context such as *Abbastanza bene, ma un po' stanco* (translating to "Pretty good, but a little tired") or *Non c'è male, grazie* (in English, "Not bad, thank you"), which can lead to longer conversations. There are also regional variations of the phrase, with many Italians asking *Come va?* ("How's it going?"), which has a similar meaning but is less personal.

Watch the Pronunciation In ***Come stai?*** the final *i* vowel must be clearly pronounced, giving the word a crisp ending. It sounds like the English *ee* in "see." If the *i* is dropped, *stai* might be mistaken for *sta*, which changes the register from informal to formal.

Complimenti INTERJECTION

(kohm-plee-MEN-tee)

Well done; Congratulations

The word ***complimenti*** is the Italian expression for "well done" or "congratulations," and it is one of the most common ways to acknowledge someone's success or effort. It is typically used to praise achievements, celebrate talents, and recognize that something has been done well. For example, if someone prepares a great meal, you might say, "***Complimenti*** *per la cena, era squisita!*" ("Well done on dinner, it was delicious!"). If a friend finishes a challenging project at work, you can express admiration by saying, "***Complimenti*** *per il tuo lavoro!*" ("Well done on your work!"). Similarly, after attending a concert, you might say to the performer, "***Complimenti***, *hai suonato benissimo!*" ("Congratulations, you played wonderfully!"). This term has its roots in the Latin word *complēre* ("to fill, to complete"). Over time, the meaning shifted from the idea of finishing something to recognizing and appreciating the outcome, which is why today ***complimenti*** carries the sense of praise and acknowledgment. This word is appropriate in both informal and formal situations. Among friends, it can sound warm and familiar, while in professional contexts it conveys respect and recognition. Overall, ***complimenti*** is more than a polite phrase: It strengthens bonds by showing genuine appreciation for others' efforts and achievements.

Da quanto tempo PHRASE

(dah KWAHN-toh TEM-poh)

How long has it been

Da quanto tempo literally translates to "since how much time" and is commonly used to ask someone how long it has been since you last saw them. This phrase often appears in friendly encounters, especially when reconnecting after a long period of time. It is more than just a phrase: It expresses surprise, happiness, and interest in another person's life. For example, if you run into an old friend unexpectedly, you might exclaim, "***Da quanto tempo*** *non ci vediamo!*" meaning "How long has it been since we've seen each other!" or you could say, "***Da quanto tempo*** *non ti vedo!*" (translating to "How long has it been since I've seen you!"). The phrase captures both joy and curiosity about the time that has passed. Breaking down the grammar, *da* is a preposition that usually means "since" or "from," *quanto* means "how much" or "how long," and *tempo* means "time." Put together, they form a way of asking about length of time, translating into "how long has it been" in English. Overall, ***da quanto tempo*** is an affectionate greeting that reflects warmth, connection, and the joy of reuniting with someone after being apart. It's usually used in informal situations with family and friends.

A Very Versatile Word In Italian, *tempo* means "time" in a general or measurable sense, but it can also mean "weather" (*Che tempo fa?* means "What's the weather like?") or "tempo or rhythm" in music and movement. Context helps you understand which meaning is intended.

Dai INTERJECTION

(dye)

Come on; Go ahead

Dai is a versatile and expressive Italian interjection that appears constantly in everyday conversation. Depending on the context, it can be translated as "come on," "go ahead," or even "no way." This flexibility makes it an indispensable part of Italian speech, reflecting the lively and playful nature of Italian interactions. One of the most common uses of ***dai*** is to encourage or motivate someone. For example, if a friend is hesitating to jump into a swimming pool, you might say, "***Dai,*** *buttati!*" (translating to "Come on, jump in!"). It can also be used to push someone toward making a decision, as in ***Dai,*** *scegli tu* ("Come on, you choose"). In these cases, the word ***dai*** serves as a gentle nudge to take action. Another important use is to express impatience, especially when someone is moving slowly. For instance, ***Dai,*** *muoviti!* means "Come on, hurry up!" Even in these contexts, the meaning of ***dai*** can range from playful to slightly demanding, depending on the tone. Finally, ***dai*** often expresses disbelief or surprise. If a friend tells you an unbelievable story, you might exclaim, "***Dai!*** *Non ci credo!*" (meaning "No way! I don't believe it!"). In this way, ***dai*** functions much like English interjections such as "No way!" or "Seriously?"

Dammi del tu PHRASE

(DAHM-mee del too)

Address me informally

Dammi del tu is the Italian expression used to invite someone to switch from the formal *Lei* to the informal *tu*. In Italian, *tu* and *Lei* are two different ways of saying "you" (in the singular form), and they reflect varying levels of social distance and familiarity. The *tu* form is informal and used among close friends, family members, and peers. It signals equality and familiarity. On the other hand, *Lei* is a formal, respectful way of addressing someone, typically used with strangers, superiors, or in professional settings. The use of *Lei* signifies a distance or a more reserved relationship. In the phrase ***dammi del tu***, the word *dammi* comes from the verb *dare* ("to give"), and *del tu* refers to the use of the informal *tu*. ***Dammi del tu*** signifies a desire to be addressed more casually and is common among colleagues and acquaintances who wish to establish a more informal rapport. For example, in a conversation, you might hear someone say, "***Dammi del tu***, *ora siamo amici!*" (translating to "Use the informal 'you' with me, now we're friends!"). In professional settings, this phrase may be used once a relationship becomes more familiar, such as after working together for a while. ***Dammi del tu*** is an important marker of personal connection in Italian culture.

Davvero ADVERB

(dahv-VEHR-roh)

Really; Truly

Davvero is a widely used and expressive word in Italian formed from *da* ("from") and *vero* ("true"), which itself derives from the Latin *verus*, meaning "true." Its core function is to emphasize truthfulness, making it a powerful way to affirm a statement or express disbelief at something surprising. ***Davvero*** appears in both casual conversations and more serious discussions. One of the most common uses of ***davvero*** is to show surprise when hearing unexpected news. For instance, if a friend tells you they are moving abroad, you might exclaim, "***Davvero?*** *Non ci posso credere!*" (translating to "Really? I can't believe it!"). In this case, the word works as a spontaneous reaction, like the English "Really?" or "Seriously?" ***Davvero*** is equally useful when you want to strengthen a statement. For example, *Questo film è* ***davvero*** *interessante* ("This film is truly interesting"). Here, ***davvero*** adds emphasis and shows that the speaker means what they say. Other examples include: *Hai fatto un lavoro* ***davvero*** *eccellente* (meaning, "You did a really excellent job") or *È* ***davvero*** *una bella giornata* (in English, "It's really a beautiful day"). Grammatically, ***davvero*** is an adverb, which means it never changes form according to gender or number.

Playing Pretend The opposite of ***davvero*** is often *per finta* ("for pretend") or *non sul serio* ("not seriously"). For example: ***Davvero*** ***ti piace?*** ("Do you really like it?"); ***No, era per finta*** ("No, I was just pretending").

Di punto in bianco PHRASE

(dee POON-toh in BYAN-koh)

All of a sudden; Out of the blue

The Italian expression ***di punto in bianco*** refers to something happening suddenly and without any warning. It captures the feeling of being caught off guard by an unexpected event. Literally, the phrase combines *di punto* ("of point") and *in bianco* ("in white"), which together do not translate naturally into English. Instead, the best equivalent is "out of the blue" or "all of a sudden," both of which express surprise and abruptness. This phrase is commonly used in everyday Italian to describe situations where events occur unexpectedly. For example, if you haven't heard from a friend in years and they suddenly get in touch, you could say, "*Luca mi ha chiamato* ***di punto in bianco*** *dopo anni di silenzio*" (translating to "Luca called me out of the blue after years of silence"). Similarly, during a meeting, if surprising news is announced, you might comment, "*La notizia è arrivata* ***di punto in bianco****, senza preavviso*" (meaning, "The news came out of the blue, without warning"). ***Di punto in bianco*** is not limited to personal interactions. It can be applied to broader contexts as well; for example, for unexpected weather events, or plot twists in a story. You might say, "*Il tempo è cambiato* ***di punto in bianco***" ("The weather changed all of a sudden"). This Italian expression emphasizes the suddenness of an event and conveys the emotional impact of being surprised when least expected.

Figurati VERB, INTERJECTION

(fee-GOOR-ah-tee)

Don't mention it; No problem

Figurati is a common Italian expression that comes from the verb *figurare*, which means "to imagine" or "to picture." In everyday conversation, ***figurati*** is most often used as a reassuring reply to dismiss the need for thanks. It conveys the idea that a favor was no trouble at all and should not be considered a burden. For example, if a friend thanks you for something small, such as holding the door open, you might simply reply with "***Figurati!***" the equivalent of "Don't mention it!" or "No problem!" in English. In other situations, such as helping a colleague with a project, you could say, "***Figurati****, è stato un piacere*" (translating to "No problem, it was a pleasure"), which emphasizes your willingness to help. ***Figurati*** is used in informal settings among friends, family, or peers, reflecting a relaxed and generous attitude. In a formal situation, this word changes from ***figurati*** to *si figuri*, the polite version that conveys the same idea but with the respect appropriate for strangers, elders, or professional situations. Both expressions highlight the Italian cultural value of politeness and generosity in daily interactions. Ultimately, whether you say ***figurati*** or *si figuri*, the message is the same: "It's no trouble at all."

Forza e coraggio PHRASE

(FOR-zah eh koh-RAH-jjoh)

Strength and courage

The Italian phrase ***forza e coraggio*** combines two powerful virtues: *forza* ("strength") and *coraggio* ("courage"). The noun *forza* can refer to both physical strength and inner resilience, while *coraggio* represents bravery. When paired together, these words create a motivating expression often used to uplift and inspire. In daily life, you might hear "***Forza e coraggio***" as encouragement when someone is facing a challenge. For example, a friend about to take an important exam might be reassured with, "*So che questo esame è difficile, ma **forza e coraggio**!*" ("I know this exam is difficult, but strength and courage!"). This phrase is also common when inspiring teamwork or solidarity. Before starting a difficult task, one might say, "***Forza e coraggio**, ce la faremo!*" ("Strength and courage, we'll make it!"), highlighting determination and unity in overcoming an obstacle. ***Forza e coraggio*** appears not only in personal conversations but also in motivational contexts, such as sports, where coaches or teammates use it to lift spirits and reinforce resilience. Culturally, ***forza e coraggio*** reflects a deeply Italian way of approaching hardship, with grit, heart, and optimism. It is less about denying difficulties and more about facing them head-on with a mixture of inner strength and determination.

Encouraging Alternatives To encourage someone, Italians also say *dai!* ("come on!"), *ce la puoi fare* ("you can do it"), *tieni duro* ("hang in there"), *in bocca al lupo* ("good luck"), and *vai così* ("keep it up").

Grazie | Grazie mille INTERJECTION

(GRAH-tsyeh) | (GRAH-tsyeh MEEL-leh)

Thank you | Thank you very much

Both ***grazie*** and ***grazie mille*** are used to express gratitude in Italian, with ***grazie*** being the standard word for "thank you" and ***grazie mille*** adding extra emphasis, translating literally to "thanks thousands." ***Grazie*** is used in everyday situations when you want to thank someone for something, from holding the door open to receiving a gift. For example, you might say, "***Grazie*** *per il caffè!*" (in English, "Thanks for the coffee!"). On the other hand, ***grazie mille*** is a more enthusiastic expression of thanks, often used when someone has gone out of their way to help you or when you want to show deeper appreciation. It's like saying "Thank you very much" or "Many thanks" in English. For instance, ***Grazie mille*** *per l'aiuto!* (translating to "Thank you very much for the help!"). This phrase is particularly common in informal settings among friends and family, though it can also be used in more formal contexts when you want to convey your gratitude in a stronger way. Both phrases reflect the Italian warmth and openness in expressing appreciation.

Tone Matters It's worth noting that ***grazie*** used with the adjective *tante* can sometimes carry an ironic tone. While ***grazie*** *tante* literally means "many thanks," Italians often use it sarcastically to express annoyance rather than gratitude. For example, if someone lets a door close in your face, you might say, "***Grazie*** *tante!*"

Magari ADVERB, INTERJECTION

(mah-GAH-ree)

I wish; If only; Maybe

Magari is one of the most versatile and expressive words in Italian, carrying different shades of meaning depending on the context. At its core, it expresses a wish or desire for something that feels unlikely to happen, much like the English phrases "I wish" or "if only." For example, if a student is struggling with a tricky grammar exercise, they might exclaim, "***Magari*** *fosse facile!*" (in English, "I wish it were easy!"). In this use, ***magari*** conveys longing for something just out of reach. However, ***magari*** is not limited to wishful thinking. In everyday conversation, it is also used more casually to express possibility, hope, or a sense of openness about the future. For instance, ***Magari*** *ci vediamo domani* means "Maybe we'll see each other tomorrow," while ***Magari*** *il tempo sarà bello!* translates to "Maybe the weather will be nice!" In these cases, the word softens uncertainty with optimism. It's useful to compare ***magari*** with *forse*, another Italian word that means "maybe." While *forse* is more neutral and factual, ***magari*** adds an emotional nuance, something closer to hope and desire. For example, *Forse verrà* ("Maybe he'll come") sounds tentative and uncertain, whereas ***Magari*** *verrà!* ("I hope he'll come!") communicates a sincere wish.

A Common Opposite The opposite of ***magari*** (expressing hope or wishful thinking) is often *purtroppo*, which conveys disappointment or an unwanted reality: ***Magari*** *potessi venire!* ("I wish I could come!") versus *Purtroppo non posso venire* ("Unfortunately I can't come").

Meno male NOUN PHRASE, INTERJECTION

(MEH-noh MAH-leh)

Thank goodness; Luckily

Meno male is a widely used Italian phrase that conveys a sense of relief, especially when something negative has been avoided or a situation turns out better than expected. Although its literal translation is "less bad," in practice it functions like the English expressions "thank goodness" or "luckily." ***Meno male*** captures the Italian tendency to focus on the positive side of an experience, even when circumstances are less than ideal. One of the most common situations where you might hear ***meno male*** is when danger or inconvenience is avoided. For example, if your flight is delayed but you still manage to make your connection, you could say, "***Meno male*** *che siamo arrivati in tempo!*" (translating to "Thank goodness we arrived on time!"). Similarly, if a child falls but isn't hurt, a parent might exclaim, "***Meno male*** *che non si è fatto male*" ("Luckily he didn't get hurt"). This phrase is also useful in everyday conversations when expressing gratitude. Imagine someone saying, "*Ha piovuto tutto il giorno, ma* ***meno male*** *che avevamo l'ombrello*" (meaning "It rained all day, but thank goodness we had an umbrella"). Because of its flexibility, ***meno male*** can be used informally with friends and family, or in professional settings when discussing outcomes at work. It is a simple, natural way to share relief and highlight a silver lining, the Italian way.

Mi raccomando VERB PHRASE

(mee rahk-koh-MAHN-doh)

Make sure to

Mi raccomando is a very common Italian phrase used to stress the importance of following through with something. While its literal meaning is "I recommend to you," the actual sense is much stronger, often closer to "make sure to." It conveys urgency and care, depending on the situation and tone of voice. For example, a parent might remind a child before leaving for school, "***Mi raccomando,*** *fai attenzione!*" (translating to "Make sure to pay attention!"). Similarly, a friend might say, "***Mi raccomando***, *chiamami appena arrivi*" (meaning "Make sure to call me as soon as you arrive"), expressing both concern and care. This phrase can range from casual reminders, like ***Mi raccomando***, *non dimenticare il tuo libro!* ("Make sure you don't forget your book!"), to more serious matters where the stakes are higher, such as exams, interviews, or important commitments. Grammatically, the phrase comes from the reflexive verb *raccomandarsi*, which means "to recommend oneself." In practice, however, ***mi raccomando*** has taken on a fixed idiomatic (culturally specific) meaning, functioning almost like an interjection rather than a literal verb phrase. Used in informal contexts, ***mi raccomando*** reflects the Italian cultural emphasis on attentiveness and responsibility. It shows not only the importance of the task but also the speaker's personal investment in the listener's well-being.

Mi tocca VERB PHRASE

(mee TOHK-kah)

It's my turn; I have to do it

Mi tocca is a common Italian expression used to indicate that it is your turn to do something or that you have to take on a task, often with some reluctance or mild annoyance. The verb *toccare* literally means "to touch," but when used with the pronoun *mi* ("to me") in this idiomatic sense, it conveys the idea of something "falling to you" or "being your responsibility." For this reason, when someone says "***Mi tocca***," they are expressing that they are the one expected or required to act, whether they want to or not. For example, you might hear, "***Mi tocca** pulire la cucina*" (translating to "It's my turn to clean the kitchen") or "***Mi tocca** andare a fare la spesa*" (meaning "I have to go grocery shopping"). In both cases, the speaker isn't necessarily enthusiastic about the task but is acknowledging that it has become their duty. In daily life, the phrase is used in households, workplaces, or group settings when responsibilities are divided. Grammatically, ***mi tocca*** is usually followed by a verb in the infinitive ("to ___") form, such as *andare* ("to go"), *fare* ("to do"), or *studiare* ("to study"). For instance, ***Mi tocca** studiare tutta la sera* means "I have to study all evening." The construction can also change pronouns; for example, *ti tocca* ("it's your turn"), *gli tocca* ("it's his turn"), and so on. Overall, ***mi tocca*** is a practical and expressive phrase that captures both obligation and emotions.

Neanche per sogno PHRASE

(neh-AHN-keh per SOHN-yoh)

Not in a million years; Not a chance

Neanche per sogno is a vivid Italian expression used to strongly refuse or deny something. Literally, it translates as "not even for dream," but in English it is best equated to "not in a million years" or "not a chance." The phrase carries a strong emotional response. For example, if a reckless friend who has already crashed their car asks to borrow yours, you might respond with, "***Neanche per sogno!***" (translating to "Not a chance!"). In another situation, if someone suggests you work all weekend without pay, you could exclaim, "***Neanche per sogno** che lo faccio!*" (meaning "Not a chance I'm doing it!"). The expression leaves no room for negotiation; it makes it very clear that the answer is firmly "no." The expression ***neanche per sogno*** creates a metaphorical image: something so impossible or undesirable that you wouldn't agree to it even in a dream. It's an informal and a bit exaggerated expression, most often used among friends, family, or peers. Beyond refusal, ***neanche per sogno*** also conveys disbelief at an unrealistic suggestion. It highlights a cultural tendency in Italian to mix seriousness with expressive, dramatic language.

Say It Right Pronunciation here is important. In ***neanche per sogno***, make sure to pronounce the "ch" in *neanche* as a hard *k*. In *sogno*, the "gn" is pronounced like the "ny" sound in the English word "canyon."

Non ci piove PHRASE

(non chee PYOH-veh)

There's no doubt about it

Non ci piove is an Italian expression used to emphasize that something is indisputable and beyond question. The imagery behind the phrase suggests that nothing can "rain" on the statement; there is no way to dispute it. ***Non ci piove*** is often used to confirm the truth of a statement. For example: ***Non ci piove*** *che lui sia il miglior cantante* (translating to "There's no doubt that he is the best singer"). Another example can be: ***Non ci piove*** *che lei abbia ragione* ("There's no doubt that she's right"). Grammatically, the phrase breaks down as *non* ("not"), *ci* ("on it"), and *piove* ("it rains," from the Italian verb *piovere*). ***Non ci piove*** carries a colloquial tone: It is used in informal settings, such as conversations with friends, family, or colleagues in relaxed contexts. In a formal context, it might come across a little direct. By using ***non ci piove***, Italian speakers add emphasis to their statements and opinions.

When It Rains It is important to note that *piovere* is an impersonal verb. In Italian, weather verbs like *piovere* do not explicitly use "it" as a subject the same way English does. Instead, the impersonal verb stands alone, and the subject "it" is not explicitly stated.

Non mi va giù PHRASE

(non mee vah JOO)

I can't accept it

Non mi va giù is an informal Italian expression that conveys the feeling that something does not sit well with you emotionally. While the literal translation is "(it) for me doesn't go down," ***non mi va giù*** describes the emotional difficulty of accepting or coming to terms with a situation. The phrase is built around the verb *andare* ("to go"), conjugated in the third-person singular form *va* ("it goes"), followed by the adverb *giù* ("down"). Together they suggest the idea of something being hard to swallow. When paired with the indirect pronoun *mi* ("for me"), the expression becomes highly personal, indicating that the speaker is directly and emotionally affected. In practice, ***non mi va giù*** is often used when something feels unfair and disappointing. For example: ***Non mi va giù*** *che mi abbiano mentito* translates as "I can't accept that they lied to me." In this case, the phrase highlights not only the fact that the person was lied to, but also the emotional weight of betrayal. Because of its strong personal nuance, the expression ***non mi va giù*** emphasizes subjectivity: It does not describe an objective truth, but rather the speaker's internal struggle. The imagery of something "not going down" resonates with the experience of finding certain realities difficult to digest, making it a powerful expression in everyday Italian.

Non si sa mai PHRASE

(non see sah MY)

Better safe than sorry; You never know

Non si sa mai is a common and practical Italian expression that conveys the idea that anything can happen and that it's best to be prepared. Literally, it translates to "not one knows never," but its meaning aligns with the English phrase "better safe than sorry." It reflects a cautious attitude, reminding people that things are never certain and precautions can make a difference. In everyday situations, Italians use this phrase frequently. For example, if the weather looks uncertain and you are unsure whether to bring an umbrella, you might say "*Meglio portarlo, **non si sa mai**!*" (translating to "Better to bring it, you never know!"). Similarly, if you are about to go on a long trip, someone might remind you, "*Porta un po' di soldi in più, **non si sa mai***" ("Bring some extra money, better safe than sorry"). Grammatically, the expression ***non si sa mai*** uses the impersonal construction *si sa* ("one knows"), paired with the negation *non* ("not") and *mai* ("ever" or "never"). Overall, ***non si sa mai*** embodies a mindset of caution mixed with practicality. It can be used in light conversations or more seriously when discussing risks.

Double Negatives Done Right In Italian, the expression ***non si sa mai*** also shows the common use of double negation (*non . . . mai*). Unlike English, Italian allows and even requires this structure, so ***non si sa mai*** literally means "not . . . never."

Per carità INTERJECTION

(per kah-ree-TAH)

For heaven's sake

Per carità is a widely used Italian expression that adds emphasis, often in situations of frustration or disbelief. Literally, it translates as "for charity," but in everyday Italian its meaning is closer to the English phrases "for heaven's sake" and "for goodness' sake." While the literal meaning is rooted in religious and moral traditions, its modern use is figurative and idiomatic. Depending on the tone of voice, it can carry a strong emotional weight. One common use is when asking someone not to do something that seems unwise or irritating. For example: ***Per carità***, *non guidare così veloce!* (translating to "For heaven's sake, don't drive so fast!"). Here, the phrase highlights the seriousness of the situation. In other cases, it can express frustration or disbelief, as in: ***Per carità***, *ma ti sembra normale?* ("For heaven's sake, does it seem normal to you?"). ***Per carità*** can also be used in a softer, more polite sense, almost like "please." For instance, if someone insists on thanking you, you might respond, "***Per carità***, *non c'è bisogno*" (translating to "Please, there's no need"). The expression ***per carità*** reflects the Italian tendency to infuse emotion and intensity into speech.

Don't Forget the Final Accent In pronunciation, remember that the word *carità* has the stress on the final *à* marked with the accent. This means you should emphasize the last syllable clearly. Without the accent, the meaning and stress would be incorrect.

Per fortuna PHRASE, INTERJECTION

(per for-TOO-nah)

Fortunately; Luckily

Per fortuna is a common Italian expression used to indicate relief, gratitude, or appreciation for a good outcome. It translates into English as "fortunately" or "luckily" and is often used when things turn out well, particularly in situations where the result could have been negative. For example, if someone avoids an accident, they might say, "***Per fortuna*** *non è successo niente!*" (translating to "Luckily, nothing happened!"). Similarly, if you arrive late to the bus stop but the bus is also running late, you might exclaim, "***Per fortuna*** *non l'ho perso*" ("Fortunately, I didn't miss it"). These examples show how this phrase expresses both relief and gratitude when circumstances work out favorably. The phrase ***per fortuna*** can also be used in more everyday, casual situations. Imagine that you bring your jacket just in case of cold wind; if the weather suddenly changes, you could say, "***Per fortuna*** *ho portato la giacca!*" (translating to "Luckily, I brought the jacket!"). This common phrase is composed of the preposition *per* ("for") and the noun *fortuna* ("fortune" or "luck"), together meaning "for luck." Overall, ***per fortuna*** is a versatile expression that reflects the Italian tendency to notice and appreciate life's fortunate turns.

> **When Luck Goes Wrong** While *fortuna* means "luck" and is part of the phrase ***per fortuna***, its opposite is *sfortuna* (sfor-TOO-nah), meaning "bad luck" or "misfortune." It is used, for example, in the common expression *che sfortuna!* (translating to "what bad luck!").

Permesso INTERJECTION

(per-MEHS-soh)

Excuse me; May I

Permesso is a polite and respectful Italian expression used when asking for permission, entering a space, or getting someone's attention. It is usually translated as "excuse me" and "may I" depending on the context. Although it comes from the verb *permettere* ("to allow" or "to permit"), in everyday conversation it functions like a stand-alone interjection, signaling courtesy and respect. One of the most common uses of ***permesso*** is when entering someone's home or a private room. Instead of simply walking in, Italians often pause at the door and say, "***Permesso****?*" the equivalent of "May I come in?" This small act reflects cultural politeness and awareness of another person's space. Another frequent context is when moving through a crowd or tight space, where you might hear, "*Mi scusi,* ***permesso****?*" (translating to "Excuse me, may I pass?"). In both cases, the word softens the action and shows consideration for others. Overall, ***permesso*** is a simple yet powerful word that embodies Italian courtesy, used in both formal and informal contexts. By using it, speakers acknowledge the presence and space of others, ensuring interactions feel respectful and considerate.

Double Consonants Done Right In ***permesso***, the double *s* should be pronounced with a longer sound. Make sure to hold the *s* slightly, almost like a brief pause, before releasing it. This distinction between single and double consonants is essential in Italian pronunciation.

Piacere NOUN, VERB, INTERJECTION

(pya-CHAY-reh)

Pleased (to meet you); To like

Piacere literally means "pleasure" in Italian, but when used during introductions, it is best translated as "Pleased to meet you." The word ***piacere*** comes from the Latin verb *placēre*, which means "to please" or "to be agreeable." Over time, it evolved into ***piacere***, keeping the core meaning of "to please." From this root, Italian developed two main uses: as a verb ("to like") and as a noun ("pleasure"). ***Piacere*** is one of the most common and polite expressions used during introductions, signaling good manners. For example, when meeting someone for the first time, you might say, "***Piacere** di conoscerti*" (translating to "Pleased to meet you") in an informal context, or "***Piacere** di conoscerLa*" when speaking formally to a stranger, elder, or professional acquaintance. Both phrases are the equivalent of "Nice to meet you" in English. In its greeting form, ***piacere*** can stand alone as a simple exclamation: "***Piacere!***" This is often accompanied by a handshake or a smile, establishing a respectful tone. Another common variation is *È stato un **piacere*** (translating to "It has been a pleasure"), typically used at the end of a meeting to politely close the interaction.

Don't Forget the "Please" Outside of introductions, ***piacere*** is also a verb meaning "to please" or "to like." When conjugated, it expresses preferences: *Mi piace la pizza* (meaning "I like pizza") or *Ti piacciono i libri?* ("Do you like books?").

Prego INTERJECTION, VERB

(PREH-go)

You are welcome; Please, go ahead

Prego is one of those little Italian words that many learners encounter right away and then keep noticing everywhere. At first, it often feels confusing because it doesn't have just one fixed meaning. Its most common use is "you are welcome," as a response to *grazie* ("thank you"). For example, if someone says, "*Grazie per il caffè*" ("Thank you for the coffee"), you would reply, "***Prego!***" But ***prego*** can do much more than that. Italians use it when offering something politely, similar to "please" in English. For example, if you invite a guest into your home, you might say, "***Prego**, entra!*" (translating to "Please, come in!"). In this sense, the word conveys friendliness and politeness. Another everyday use of ***prego*** is to encourage someone to go ahead with a request or action. In a shop, if you approach the counter and the clerk says, "***Prego***," it means "Go ahead, I'm listening." It works almost like "How can I help you?" Because of its versatility, ***prego*** can feel like a polite filler word, something Italians sprinkle into their interactions. The origin of ***prego*** lies in the verb *pregare*, meaning "to pray" or "to beg." Over time, it evolved from a formal plea into a polite everyday courtesy.

When Does It Change? When used as a verb, ***prego*** is the first-person present tense ("I pray"). The verb still changes normally: ***prego***, *preghi*, *prega*, *preghiamo*, but the fixed polite ***prego*** ("you are welcome") stays unchanged in everyday use.

Pronto INTERJECTION

(PROHN-toh)

Hello; Ready

Pronto is the standard Italian greeting used when answering the phone. Literally, the word means "ready," and the implication is "I'm ready to listen" or "I'm ready to talk." When the phone rings, instead of saying "Hello" as in English, Italians typically answer with a bright "***Pronto?***" to signal that they are present and prepared for the conversation. This usage is unique to phone conversations. You would not normally greet someone in person by saying "***Pronto***"; it's reserved almost entirely for phone calls. In daily life, if you hear ***pronto*** outside of phone use, it usually carries its literal sense of "ready," such as: *Sei **pronto**?* (translating to "Are you ready?"). The phone greeting has become such a fixed convention in Italian that it is expected in both casual and formal contexts. Whether you're talking to a close friend or answering a professional call, ***pronto*** works in all situations. The origin of this expression reflects the early days of telephones in Italy. Operators and callers would say "***Pronto***" to confirm that the line was working and that they were "ready" to proceed. Over time, this habit solidified into a universal greeting. Today, ***pronto*** remains one of the most recognizable markers of Italian phone culture: short, clear, and instantly understood.

Why Say *Pronto* at the Table? At the table, ***pronto*** is used to signal that everyone is ready to start eating or to receive food. It's a practical and very common call: ***pronto!*** ("ready to eat!").

Roba da matti PHRASE

(ROH-bah dah MAHT-tee)

That's crazy; That's madness

Roba da matti is a colorful Italian expression that literally translates to "stuff for madmen." The phrase combines the noun *roba* (meaning "stuff" or "things") with *da matti* ("for madmen"). Despite the literal meaning, it's about situations, behaviors, or events that are so out of the ordinary they seem unbelievable. Italians use ***roba da matti*** to highlight something bizarre and exaggerated; a moment that leaves you shaking your head in disbelief. For example, if a friend tells you a wild story about getting three parking tickets in one day and then bumping into another car, you might respond, "***Roba da matti!***" meaning "That's crazy!" Similarly, if someone is describing outrageous prices or shocking news, this phrase captures the sense of "That's madness!" in English. One of the interesting features of ***roba da matti*** is its flexibility. The tone can shift depending on context: Sometimes it conveys annoyance or frustration, like when bureaucracy becomes unbearable, while in other cases it expresses amazement at something so unusual it seems almost unreal. It works well in casual conversations among friends or in more dramatic storytelling; however, it's usually not used in a formal setting. In essence, ***roba da matti*** is an emphatic reaction, a way of underlining just how extreme or unbelievable something is.

Salve INTERJECTION

(SAHL-veh)

Hello; Good day

Salve is a polite and somewhat formal way of saying "hello" or "good day" in Italian, both as a greeting and farewell. Unlike the casual *ciao*, which you might use with friends and family, ***salve*** is often said when addressing someone you don't know very well, when entering a store, or in professional situations where you want to be courteous. For example, when greeting a shopkeeper or meeting a colleague for the first time, you might say, "***Salve!***" The tone of ***salve*** is interesting because it is more formal than *ciao* but less time-specific than greetings like *buongiorno* ("good morning") or *buonasera* ("good evening"). This flexibility makes it useful throughout the day, regardless of the time. It can also serve as a neutral middle ground: polite enough for formal settings, yet still warm enough to feel approachable. Although younger Italians often prefer *ciao* or time-based greetings, ***salve*** is still common in many regions of Italy, especially in central and southern areas, where it remains part of everyday politeness. The word itself comes from the Latin *salvēre*, meaning "to be well" or "to be in good health." Over centuries, it carried forward into modern Italian as the courteous greeting and farewell heard today.

Scusi | Scusa INTERJECTION, VERB

(SKOO-zee) | (SKOO-zah)

Excuse me; I'm sorry; I beg your pardon

Scusi is one of the most useful and polite words you can learn in Italian. It functions as both an apology and a way of politely getting someone's attention, especially in formal contexts. The origin of ***scusi*** traces back to the Latin *excusāre*, meaning "to free from blame" or "to make an excuse." In everyday situations, ***scusi*** is often used when you need to interrupt or approach someone respectfully. For example, in a restaurant you might say, "***Scusi***, *posso avere il menù?*" (translating to "Excuse me, may I have the menu?"). It also works as a polite way to apologize for minor inconveniences, like accidentally bumping into someone on a crowded street: *Oh,* ***scusi****!* meaning, "Oh, I'm sorry!" Additionally, ***scusi*** can be used with the meaning of "I beg your pardon" when something is not understood. It's important to note that ***scusi*** is the formal version, used with strangers, elders, or in professional settings. The informal equivalent is ***scusa***, which you would use with friends, family, or peers. There is also *mi* ***scusi*** (meaning "excuse me"), which makes the expression even more polite by using the pronoun *mi*. *Mi* ***scusi*** is very common in customer service interactions.

What Verb Form Is This? Both ***scusa*** and ***scusi*** are in the imperative because you're literally making a request: "Excuse me" or "Forgive me." Italian uses the imperative command form to ask for attention or pardon, though in this case the tone is courteous, not forceful.

Senza ombra di dubbio PHRASE

(SEN-zah OHM-brah dee DOOB-byoh)

Without a shadow of a doubt

Senza ombra di dubbio is a powerful Italian expression used to emphasize complete certainty. Literally, it means "without shadow of doubt" and also translates to "without question." It is often used when you want to eliminate any hesitation and make it clear that what you are saying is absolutely true. For example, you might say, "***Senza ombra di dubbio***, *lei è la candidata perfetta per questo lavoro*" (translating to "Without a shadow of a doubt, she is the perfect candidate for this job"). In casual conversation, it can also be used to stress strong opinions: ***Senza ombra di dubbio***, *la pizza napoletana è la migliore del mondo!* (meaning "Without a shadow of a doubt, Neapolitan pizza is the best in the world!"). The expression is flexible and can appear in both spoken and written Italian, ranging from everyday language to more formal contexts, such as journalism or academic writing. Culturally, Italians often favor vivid, metaphorical language, and ***senza ombra di dubbio*** fits perfectly into this tradition. It is stronger than simply saying *sicuramente* ("surely") or *certamente* ("certainly"), because it conveys not only certainty but the total absence of doubt.

One Word, Two Meanings In Italian, *ombra* means both "shade" and "shadow." It can refer to protection from the sun (*all'ombra degli alberi*, which translates to "in the shade of the trees") or a dark shape caused by light (*l'ombra di una persona*, which translates to "the shadow of a person"). Context tells you which meaning is intended.

Si fa per dire PHRASE

(see fah per DEE-reh)

Just saying

Si fa per dire is an Italian phrase used to clarify that something should not be taken literally. It closely parallels the English "just saying." The phrase helps soften statements that might otherwise be misunderstood or taken too seriously. For example, imagine someone saying, "***Si fa per dire***, *ma potremmo trasferirci tutti in montagna*" (meaning, "Just saying, but we could all move to the mountains"). The speaker isn't proposing an actual plan, instead, the statement is meant as a light remark. Similarly, in conversation about an impossible challenge, one might say, "***Si fa per dire***, *ma risolvere questo problema è come scalare l'Everest*" (translating to "I'm just saying, but solving this problem is like climbing Everest"). ***Si fa per dire*** appears in informal contexts, helping maintain a friendly tone while avoiding misunderstandings. This phrase is made of the impersonal construction *si fa* ("one does") combined with the verb *dire* ("to say"). Literally, it translates as "one does for say." Over time, this structure evolved into a fixed expression, emphasizing the act of speaking rather than the truth of the statement.

Let's Talk Pronunciation The pronunciation of ***si fa per dire*** is smooth and evenly paced, with each vowel produced clearly, as is typical in Italian. The stress falls on the only vowels of *si*, *fa*, and *per* and on the first syllable of *dire*, giving the phrase a rhythmic and balanced flow.

Stammi bene PHRASE

(STAHM-mee BEH-neh)

Take care

Stammi bene is a warm, informal Italian expression used to say "take care" when parting ways. The phrase comes from the verb *stare* ("to stay"), the pronoun *mi* ("for me"), and the adverb *bene* ("well"), so its literal meaning is "stay for me well." The presence of *mi* is especially significant, since it adds a personal nuance. Rather than simply wishing someone to "stay well," the phrase suggests, "Do me the favor of staying well." This construction emphasizes the closeness between the speaker and the listener. While simple, ***stammi bene*** conveys a genuine sense of care for the other person's well-being. This phrase is used among friends, relatives, or other people you feel close to. For example, after meeting a friend for coffee, you might say, "*Ciao, **stammi bene**!*" (translating to "Bye, take care!"). It creates a friendly, personal closing that shows you are thinking about the other person even after the conversation ends. Unlike more neutral goodbyes such as *arrivederci* (meaning "goodbye") or *ci vediamo* (meaning "see you"), ***stammi bene*** adds an affectionate touch. Although common in spoken Italian, ***stammi bene*** is not used in formal contexts. In professional settings, you would instead choose more standard closings such as *arrivederci* ("goodbye").

Simple Opposites The opposite of *bene* ("well") is *male* ("unwell"). You'll hear it often in everyday Italian: *Sto bene* ("I am well") versus *Sto male* ("I am unwell").

Tanto di cappello PHRASE

(*TAHN-toh dee kahp-PEL-loh*)

Hats off

Tanto di cappello is a common Italian expression that literally translates to "lots of hat." It's used to show admiration, respect, or appreciation for someone's achievements, similar to the English phrase "hats off." By saying it, you recognize another person's effort or success, giving them a kind of verbal bow. For example, if a colleague completes a difficult project ahead of schedule, you might want to say, "***Tanto di cappello*** *per quello che hai fatto!*" ("Hats off to what you did!"). Likewise, if a friend accomplishes something impressive, like running a marathon or earning a promotion, ***tanto di cappello*** conveys admiration and respect in an enthusiastic way. The phrase works in both informal and semi-formal contexts. Among friends, it shows genuine praise; in professional settings, it highlights success without sounding too casual. It's more expressive than simply saying *bravo* or *complimenti*. The origin of this idiom goes back to the long-standing custom of removing one's hat as a sign of respect or honor. Saying ***tanto di cappello*** is like verbally enacting that gesture, taking off your hat, emphatically "a lot." Today, ***tanto di cappello*** remains a vivid, respectful way to celebrate someone's success and give credit where it is due.

One Letter Makes the Difference In Italian, *capello* means "a strand of hair" (on your head), while *cappello* (with double *p*) means "hat." The double consonant changes both meaning and pronunciation.

Ti voglio bene PHRASE

(tee VOHL-yoh BEH-neh)

I love you; I care for you

Ti voglio bene is one of the most common Italian expressions of affection. While it can be translated as "I love you" or "I care for you," it is used in less romantic contexts than *ti amo* (that is, "I love you" to a romantic partner). ***Ti voglio bene*** conveys warmth and genuine affection in relationships with family members, friends, or people you care about without romantic implications. For example, a child might say, "***Ti voglio bene,*** *mamma!*" (translating to "I love you, Mom!"), or you might tell a close friend, "***Ti voglio bene,*** *amico mio!*" ("I care for you, my friend!"). In these contexts, the phrase expresses a bond of love and appreciation. ***Ti voglio bene*** literally means "To you (I) want well" and it conveys the idea of wanting what is good for someone. In contrast, *ti amo* is reserved almost exclusively for romantic partners and carries a more passionate weight. Ultimately, ***ti voglio bene*** highlights the Italian emphasis on expressing care openly. It's a phrase that strengthens relationships, reminding those around you that they are valued and held close to the heart.

Going Plural In addition to ***ti voglio bene***, Italians also use *vi voglio bene* when addressing more than one person. For example, a parent might say it to their children, "*Vi voglio bene, bambini*" ("I love you, kids"). This plural form carries the same affection but is directed at a group rather than an individual.

Uffa INTERJECTION

(OOF-fah)

Ugh; How annoying

Uffa is a very common Italian interjection used to express annoyance, impatience, or frustration. It functions much like the English "ugh," or "how annoying." Italians typically use it when they feel irritated, fed up, or bored. For example, if you are stuck in traffic, you might exclaim, "***Uffa***, *che traffico!*" ("Ugh, what traffic!"). Or if you are waiting in a long line, you might say, "***Uffa***, *che noia!*" ("Ugh, how boring!"). The expression conveys mild exasperation, but its meaning depends heavily on tone of voice. When said softly, ***uffa*** may sound playful, while when shouted, it can show genuine irritation. This flexibility makes it a favorite expression in everyday informal contexts with friends and family. Grammatically, ***uffa*** is an interjection, so it stands alone and never changes form. It's short, simple, and effective, allowing speakers to communicate emotion instantly without the need for extra words. As for its origin, ***uffa*** is considered onomatopoeic, imitating the sound of a long sigh of frustration. In terms of pronunciation, pay special attention to the double *f*, which should be held slightly longer than a single *f*. Stretching the consonant and producing a longer sound gives the word its emphatic, sigh-like quality. Properly pronounced, ***uffa*** perfectly captures that universal feeling of annoyance.

Volentieri ADVERB

(voh-len-TYEH-ree)

Gladly; With pleasure

Volentieri is a positive and versatile Italian adverb that expresses willingness, eagerness, or pleasure in doing something. It translates as "gladly," "with pleasure," or even "sure" depending on context. Italians often use it as a warm and enthusiastic response when accepting invitations, offering help, or agreeing to participate in an activity. For example, if a friend asks, "*Vuoi venire a prendere un caffè?*" ("Do you want to go for a coffee?"), you could reply simply with "***Volentieri!***" ("Gladly!"). Similarly, if someone requests your assistance, you might say, "*Ti aiuto* ***volentieri***" (translating to "I'll gladly help you"). The word conveys not only agreement but also enthusiasm, showing that you are happy to accept rather than reluctantly agreeing. Grammatically, ***volentieri*** is an adverb, which means it does not change form based on gender or number. This makes it easy to use in all contexts, whether the subject is singular or plural. It modifies the action itself, emphasizing the pleasure or willingness behind it. The origin of ***volentieri*** can be traced to the Latin word *voluntāriē,* meaning "willing" or "voluntarily." Over time, it developed into ***volentieri***. In terms of pronunciation, the stress falls on the e in the syllable "tie." ***Volentieri*** is an excellent phrase to make interactions sound friendly and inviting.

4

Food and Fun

In Italy, food and fun naturally go together. A meal is never just about eating, it's about sharing laughter, stories, and moments that bring people closer. Saying *Buon appetito* or calling out *A tavola!* is an open invitation to connect. Words like *aperitivo* and phrases like *a km zero* reveal cherished traditions and personal values. From Sunday lunches that stretch into the afternoon, to evening strolls for *gelato*, in Italy food is a way to celebrate life. In this chapter, you'll discover the fun for yourself, exploring the origins and delicious details of words like *antipasto* and phrases like *cin cin*! Learning these expressions lets you have a delicious taste of Italy: its joy, and the everyday magic found around the table.

A km zero PHRASE

(ah kee-LOH-meh-troh ZEHR-oh)

Locally sourced

A km zero, meaning "at zero kilometers," is an Italian expression that celebrates local production and short supply chains. It refers to food, wine, or other products that are grown, made, and consumed within the same region, minimizing transportation and environmental impact. The English equivalent would be "locally sourced" or "farm-to-table." You'll often see this phrase on restaurant menus or market signs, such as *prodotti **a km zero*** ("locally sourced products"), indicating ingredients that come directly from nearby farms. Italians use it to emphasize freshness, quality, and a close relationship between producer and consumer. For example, you could hear someone say, "*Io preferisco comprare frutta **a km zero***" (translating to "I prefer to buy locally sourced fruit"). Beyond food, the idea also represents a broader philosophy of mindful consumption and sustainability. Choosing ***a km zero*** supports small local businesses, preserves traditional methods, and reduces pollution caused by transport. The concept emerged in the early 2000s alongside Italy's growing environmental movement and has since become a mark of pride for restaurants and shops that promote regional products. ***A km zero*** expresses a lifestyle that values community, care for the planet, and the simple pleasure of eating what the land nearby provides.

A occhio e croce PHRASE

(ah OHK-kyoh eh KROH-cheh)

Roughly; By approximation

A occhio e croce is a popular Italian idiom meaning "roughly" or "by approximation." The phrase is common in the kitchen. A cook might say, "***A occhio e croce*** *ci vuole un po' di sale in più*" ("By eye, it needs a bit more salt"). Literally translated as "by eye and cross," it describes making an estimate without exact measurement, relying instead on intuition and quick observation. Italians use it frequently in everyday speech to give an approximate amount, number, or distance. For example, you might also hear someone say, "***A occhio e croce*** *saranno cinquanta persone*" (translating to "There will be roughly fifty people") or "***A occhio e croce*** *ci vorranno venti minuti*" ("It'll take about twenty minutes"). It captures a blend of practicality and instinct, trusting one's eye rather than a calculator. This expression has ancient roots connected to the craft of weaving. It originates from the Latin *ad oculum* (meaning "by eye") and refers to when old weavers repaired a broken thread. They would pass the new thread through the fabric several times, recreating a small cross by eye, ***a occhio e croce***, without tools, trusting only their skill and judgment. The result wasn't perfectly precise, but it worked well enough.

A tavola PHRASE

(ah TAH-voh-lah)

To the table

A tavola literally means "at table," but in Italian culture, it carries a meaning that goes far beyond the physical table itself. It represents togetherness and the joy of sharing a meal. When Italians say, "***A tavola!***," it's not just a call to eat, it's an invitation to gather, to pause the day's rush, and to connect with others. A parent might call out, "***A tavola,*** *bambini!*" (translating to "To the table, kids!"), signaling that it's time for food and family. Meals in Italy are important moments of connection, not hurried stops between tasks. Sitting ***a tavola*** means being present, engaging in conversation, and celebrating food. There's even a beloved Italian saying, "***A tavola*** *non si invecchia,*" in English "You do not grow old at the table." It expresses the idea that time seems to stop when you're surrounded by good food and good company. Whether it's a long Sunday lunch, a simple weeknight dinner, or a festive holiday meal, ***a tavola*** embodies the Italian philosophy that nourishment is not just for the body but also for the soul.

Table versus Table In Italian, *tavolo* and *tavola* both mean "table," but they're used in different contexts. The word *tavolo* refers to the physical piece of furniture; for example, *Il tavolo è di legno* ("The table is made of wood"). The word *tavola*, on the other hand, refers to the table as a social or symbolic space, especially when set for a meal.

Acqua frizzante NOUN PHRASE

(AHK-kwah friz-ZAN-teh)

Sparkling water

Acqua frizzante means "sparkling water," one of the two main choices when ordering water in Italy. The other is *acqua naturale*, or "still water." Waiters almost always ask, "*Acqua naturale o frizzante?*" (translating to "Still or sparkling water?"). The word *frizzante* comes from the verb *frizzare*, meaning "to fizz," capturing the lively bubbles that make sparkling water refreshing. Italians typically enjoy ***acqua frizzante*** chilled, especially during meals, as the carbonation is believed to cleanse the palate and complement food. In restaurants, water is almost always served in bottles rather than from the tap, and ordering it politely is easy. You would say, "*Vorrei una bottiglia di* ***acqua frizzante****, per favore*" (translating to "I would like a bottle of sparkling water, please"). This phrase is simple yet deeply woven into Italian dining culture, where even water is chosen with intention. While many prefer *acqua naturale*, ***acqua frizzante*** remains a favorite for its crisp, effervescent taste.

Why No Free Water? In Italy, water is almost never served for free in restaurants. Instead of tap water, restaurants order bottled *acqua naturale* or ***acqua frizzante***, which is added to your bill. Free refills are uncommon, and each new bottle must be purchased separately. This reflects both cultural tradition and Italy's strong preference for quality bottled water.

Antipasto NOUN

(ahn-tee-PAH-stoh)

Appetizer

Antipasto means "appetizer" and refers to the first course of a traditional Italian meal, served before the main dishes. This term comes from the Latin *ante* ("before") and Italian *pasto* ("meal"), literally meaning "before meal." In Italy, the ***antipasto*** sets the tone for the dining experience, inviting conversation before the main courses begin. A typical ***antipasto*** might include a selection of cured meats such as *prosciutto crudo* ("raw cured ham"), *salame* ("cured sausage"), or *bresaola* ("air-dried salted beef"), paired with cheeses like mozzarella, *parmigiano* ("Parmesan"), or *pecorino* ("sheep's milk cheese"). It often features marinated vegetables, *peperoni grigliati* ("grilled peppers"), *melanzane sott'olio* ("eggplant preserved in oil"), and *carciofini* ("baby artichokes"), as well as olives and bread. In Italian restaurants, sharing *un* ***antipasto*** *misto* ("a mixed appetizer plate") marks the joyful beginning of a meal, especially on Sundays or holidays. ***Antipasto*** often represents regional pride, as each area often highlights its specialties, from Tuscan *crostini di fegatini* ("small toasted bread rounds topped with liver pâté") to Sicilian *caponata* ("sweet and sour relish made with eggplant, celery, olives, and capers"). More than just food, ***antipasto*** embodies the Italian way of savoring life, slowly.

Using *Pasto* Like an Italian **The word *pasto* in Italian means "meal." The phrase *fare un pasto veloce* means "to have a quick meal," while *pasto completo* describes a full meal with several courses.**

Aperitivo NOUN

(ah-peh-ree-TEE-voh)

Predinner drink

Aperitivo is a beloved Italian tradition that takes place before dinner, typically between 6 p.m. and 8 p.m. More than just a drink, it's a cultural ritual that blends conversation and taste. The word ***aperitivo*** comes from the Latin *aperīre*, meaning "to open," symbolizing the idea of "opening the stomach" in preparation for the meal to come. It's a transition between the workday and the evening, inviting people to slow down and enjoy the moment. Typical *aperitivi* (plural form) include light, slightly bitter drinks that stimulate the appetite, such as Aperol Spritz, Campari Soda, Negroni, or a glass of prosecco. These are often accompanied by small bites known as *stuzzichini*, like olives, chips, nuts, or mini sandwiches. In many bars, where ***aperitivo*** is served, especially in northern Italy, it may come with an abundant buffet of savory snacks, turning it into a mini feast known as *apericena* (a blend of ***aperitivo*** and *cena*, or "dinner"). The experience is less about the food or drink itself and more about community and atmosphere. Meeting friends and saying, "*Ci vediamo per un **aperitivo**?*" (translating to "Shall we meet for an aperitivo?") captures the Italian spirit of connection. Ultimately, ***aperitivo*** is the perfect mix of taste, leisure, and togetherness that defines the Italian art of living well.

How Much Does It Cost? In Italy, ***aperitivo*** usually costs €5–10 for a drink, often including small snacks. In bigger cities or trendy spots, it can reach €12–15, especially if it comes with a generous food spread.

Bruschetta NOUN

(broo-SKEHT-tah)

Toasted bread with tomatoes

Bruschetta is a classic Italian starter made of toasted bread rubbed with garlic and topped with olive oil, tomatoes, or other fresh ingredients. The word comes from the Roman dialect verb *bruscare*, meaning "to toast" or "to burn slightly," referring to the rustic practice of grilling bread over an open fire. Traditionally, the bread is drizzled with extra-virgin olive oil and seasoned with a pinch of salt, creating a simple yet deeply flavorful bite. The most beloved version is ***bruschetta*** *al pomodoro* (literally in English, "at tomato"): toasted bread topped with diced ripe tomatoes, fresh basil, olive oil, and a touch of garlic. Each ingredient is chosen for freshness and quality. The pronunciation often confuses non-Italians: ***bruschetta*** is pronounced with a hard *k* sound, because in Italian the combination "ch" produces that sound. Across Italy, ***bruschetta*** varies by region. In Tuscany, it's often called *fettunta* and served plain with olive oil; in southern regions, it might include anchovies, olives, or roasted peppers. Served in restaurants and at family gatherings, ***bruschetta*** represents the beauty of turning everyday ingredients into something extraordinary. It's a celebration of good bread, good olive oil, and the Italian art of savoring simplicity.

Buon appetito PHRASE

(bwohn ahp-peh-TEE-toh)

Enjoy your meal

Buon appetito means "enjoy your meal" and is one of the most familiar and heartwarming Italian expressions. It's said just before eating to wish others a pleasant meal, showing care, gratitude, and good manners. In Italy, meals are moments of connection, so saying "***Buon appetito!***" is a way to honor the food and the people sharing it. Families and friends often say it together before the first bite, almost like a ritual that signals the beginning of a shared experience. The phrase comes from *buon* ("good") and *appetito* ("appetite"), literally meaning "good appetite." A typical exchange might be a round of ***Buon appetito*** *a tutti!* (translating to "Enjoy your meal, everyone!"). It's not just a polite phrase; it is a small expression of community and appreciation for the cook's effort. In restaurants, servers may also say, "***Buon appetito!***" when bringing dishes to the table, emphasizing Italy's culture of hospitality and enjoyment of food. Since it is a fixed expression, ***buon appetito*** does not change its ending whether you are speaking to one single person or to more people. Around every Italian table, ***buon appetito*** is both a greeting and a celebration of good food, good company, and the simple pleasure of dining together.

Caffè corretto NOUN PHRASE

(kahf-FEH kor-RET-toh)

Espresso with a splash of liquor

Caffè corretto literally means "corrected coffee," and it refers to an espresso "corrected" or "improved" with a small splash of liquor, most commonly *grappa*, *sambuca*, or occasionally brandy. The *corretto* humorously implies that regular coffee needs a little something extra to be "set right." It's an Italian ritual, especially after a meal, enjoyed as a digestif that combines the boldness of espresso with spirits. When ordering in Italy, you might say, "*Prendo un* ***caffè corretto***," translating to "I'll have an espresso with liquor." This tradition has deep roots in Italian coffee culture. In the colder northern regions, ***caffè corretto*** is particularly popular during winter months, offering both caffeine and warmth in a single sip. Each region and person may have a preferred "correction." For example, ***caffè corretto*** *alla grappa* (espresso with *grappa*) in Veneto or ***caffè corretto*** *alla sambuca* (espresso with *sambuca*) more common in central and southern Italy. The liquor is usually added just enough to enhance the flavor without overpowering the coffee's aroma. Beyond being a drink, ***caffè corretto*** captures a cultural moment and is often enjoyed at the bar counter. In some areas, bartenders serve the espresso and liquor separately, allowing you to "correct" the coffee yourself. Ultimately, ***caffè corretto*** is a small ritual of indulgence and refinement. It celebrates the Italian art of transforming something as simple as coffee into a new and different experience.

Cannolo NOUN

(kahn-NOH-loh)

Sicilian pastry with ricotta filling

A ***cannolo*** is one of Sicily's most iconic and beloved desserts: a crisp, golden pastry shell filled with smooth and sweet ricotta cream. The name comes from *canna*, meaning "reed," because the original shells were wrapped around small river reed tubes before being fried to give them their characteristic cylindrical shape. Today, metal tubes are used instead, though the technique remains the same. The plural form is *cannoli*, used when referring to more than one. For example, *Vorrei un* ***cannolo*** *per favore* means "I would like one cannolo please." Meanwhile, *Vorrei due cannoli per favore,* translates to "I would like two cannoli please." Traditionally, the filling is made from fresh sheep's milk ricotta, sweetened with sugar and often mixed with chocolate chips, candied orange peel, or chopped pistachios. Just before serving, the ends are usually decorated with crushed nuts or candied fruit and dusted lightly with powdered sugar. The contrast between the crispy shell and creamy filling creates a perfect balance of textures and flavors. The ***cannolo*** originated in Caltanissetta and has deep cultural roots in Sicilian history. It is said that it was first created in a convent during the Arab domination of the island, symbolizing abundance and celebration. Over the centuries, the ***cannolo*** evolved into a pastry enjoyed during Carnival and later became a year-round treat. Today, the ***cannolo*** is a symbol of Sicilian creativity, hospitality, and joy.

Cappuccino NOUN

(kahp-poo-CHEE-noh)

Coffee with steamed milk

Cappuccino is one of Italy's most iconic and beloved coffee drinks, made from a perfect balance of espresso and steamed milk. It's typically enjoyed in the morning, often paired with a fresh *cornetto* (Italian croissant), as part of the typical Italian breakfast. A typical request at the bar is simply, "*Un **cappuccino**, per favore*" (translating to "One cappuccino, please"), often enjoyed standing at the counter while chatting with the barista. The name ***cappuccino*** comes from the Capuchin monks (*frati cappuccini*) of Italy, whose brown robes resemble the warm color of espresso when mixed with milk. The creamy layer of milk on top not only softens the espresso's intensity but also gives the drink its signature smooth texture. In Italy, ***cappuccino*** is considered a morning ritual, not an all-day beverage. Italians rarely drink it after 11 a.m., as milk-based coffees are thought to be too heavy to consume later in the day. Ordering ***cappuccino*** after lunch or dinner would usually mark you as a tourist. Instead, Italians switch to *caffè espresso* for a post-meal pick-me-up. Beyond its ingredients, the ***cappuccino*** represents the Italian love for ritual and simplicity.

Similar Words, Different Things In Italian, *cappuccio* means a "hood or cover," while ***cappuccino*** is the coffee drink with milk. They share the same root, referring to the hooded Capuchin monks, but one is clothing-related, the other is coffee.

Castagne NOUN

(kahs-TAH-nyeh)

Chestnuts

Castagne are chestnuts (*castagna*, in the singular form), one of the most popular symbols of autumn in Italy. These brown nuts have been a staple in Italian cuisine for centuries, once serving as an essential food for rural families in remote regions. Versatile and nourishing, ***castagne*** can be roasted, boiled, or transformed into flour for desserts. A classic Italian expression of their flavor is *castagnaccio*, a dense, slightly sweet cake made from chestnut flour, olive oil, pine nuts, and raisins. It is an ancient Tuscan recipe that reflects simplicity and tradition. Another popular dessert is *marron glacé*, chestnuts candied in syrup, often enjoyed during the holidays as a refined treat. You might hear someone say, "*Abbiamo comprato le **castagne** al mercato*" (translating to "We bought chestnuts at the market"). Perhaps the most iconic way to enjoy ***castagne*** is as *caldarroste*: roasted chestnuts sold by street vendors in paper cones. Cooked over open flames, they release a smoky, sweet aroma that will warm up your hands during cold winter days. In towns and cities across Italy, sharing *caldarroste* is more than a snack; it's a ritual of connection bringing people together in city squares. ***Castagne*** along with their unique flavor remind Italians of home and gathering around simple food.

That Tricky "GN" Sound In ***castagne***, the "gn" sound is pronounced similarly to the "ny" in "canyon." It's one smooth sound: *-gne (nyeh)*.

Cenone di Capodanno NOUN PHRASE

(cheh-NOH-neh dee kah-poh-DAHN-noh)

New Year's Eve dinner

Cenone di Capodanno refers to the grand feast held on the final night of the year. The word *cenone* is the augmentative form (a word that's modified to emphasize its size and importance) of *cena*, or "dinner." *Cenone* is not just any meal; it is the meal of the year. Italians celebrate it with family and friends, gathering around long tables filled with dishes and anticipation for the year to come. It's a time when food, tradition, and hope all blend into one joyful evening. Typical dishes vary by region but share a common theme of abundance. You might hear that "*Il* ***Cenone di Capodanno*** *è una tradizione importante in Italia*," meaning "New Year's Eve dinner is an important tradition in Italy." The meal usually lasts for hours, beginning late in the evening and continuing past midnight. At midnight, Italians toast with sparkling *spumante* or prosecco, exchange warm wishes or *auguri*, and often step outside to watch *fuochi d'artificio* ("fireworks"). Some also observe old superstitions, like wearing red underwear for luck or throwing old objects out the window to symbolically let go of the past. More than a meal, the ***Cenone di Capodanno*** is a celebration of renewal that captures the Italian way of ending the year, surrounded by good food and loved ones.

A Very Italian New Year ***Capodanno*** **means New Year's Day or New Year's celebrations. It literally comes from** ***capo*** **("head") and** ***anno*** **("year"), meaning the start of the year.**

Cicchetti NOUN

(cheek-KEHT-tee)

Small Venetian appetizers

Cicchetti are small, savory bites typical of Venice, often compared to Spanish tapas but uniquely Venetian in flavor. These little dishes are served in traditional bars known as *bacari* (singular *bacaro*), where locals stop throughout the day to enjoy food, wine, and conversation. Sometimes spelled *cicheti* in Venetian dialect, ***cicchetti*** can include tiny toasts topped with seafood, marinated vegetables, cured meats, or cheeses. Each *cicchetto* is designed to be eaten in one or two bites, paired with a glass of local wine or an *ombra* (literally "shadow," the Venetian term for a small glass of house wine). To experience Venetian life at its most authentic, locals and visitors take part in *un giro di* ***cicchetti*** (that is, a "cicchetti crawl") moving from one *bacaro* to another, sampling different specialties along the way. Popular examples include *crostini con baccalà mantecato* ("creamed cod on toast"), *sarde in saor* ("sweet-and-sour sardines"), and *uova con acciughe* ("eggs with anchovies"). Each *bacaro* has its own unique offerings, reflecting Venice's rich culinary heritage. The tradition of ***cicchetti*** dates back centuries, when workers and merchants would share small snacks with wine during breaks along the canals. Today, it remains a beloved ritual that captures the essence of Venetian culture: social and full of flavor.

Cin cin INTERJECTION

(cheen cheen)

Cheers

Cin cin is the Italian expression for "cheers," joyfully used when clinking glasses during a toast. It's pronounced with a soft "ch" sound (as in "church") at the beginning of each word. Italians say ***cin cin*** to celebrate special occasions. A common toast is ***Cin cin*** *alla tua salute!* meaning "Cheers to your health!" It is a wish for well-being. It's believed that ***cin cin*** comes from the sound glasses make when they gently touch during a toast. Etiquette encourages making eye contact while saying ***cin cin*** and taking a sip immediately afterward as a sign of respect. Whether celebrating a wedding, a casual dinner, or an evening *aperitivo*, ***cin cin*** embodies the Italian art of enjoying the present moment. It's a simple yet meaningful way to express gratitude and joy. With every ***cin cin***, Italians raise not just their glasses but their spirits, toasting to life.

Contorno NOUN

(kon-TOR-noh)

Side dish

Contorno means "side dish" in Italian and refers to the foods served alongside the second course, or *secondo piatto*, to complete a balanced meal. Typically, *contorni* (plural form) consist of vegetables, either cooked, grilled, or raw, but they can also include potatoes, legumes, or simple salads. The term comes from the verb *contornare*, meaning "to surround," reflecting the idea that the side dish "goes around" or accompanies the main plate, enhancing its flavor. In a traditional Italian meal, the ***contorno*** follows the *primo* ("first course," usually pasta or risotto) and is served with the *secondo* (meat or fish). Common examples of **contorno** include *patate al forno* ("roasted potatoes"), *spinaci saltati in padella* ("sautéed spinach"), *verdure grigliate* ("grilled vegetables"), or *insalata di pomodori* ("tomato salad"). Each **contorno** is prepared using high-quality ingredients and minimal seasoning, often just olive oil, salt, and a squeeze of lemon to allow natural flavors to shine. You might say, "*Vorrei un* ***contorno*** *di verdure, per favore*" (translating to "I'd like a side of vegetables, please") when ordering at a restaurant. Italians value the ***contorno*** as more than just an addition. It's a fundamental part of the meal that provides nutritional balance. Light and crisp or warm and comforting, the ***contorno*** transforms a course into a complete experience.

Coperto NOUN

(koh-PER-toh)

Cover charge

Coperto is a small charge added to the bill in many Italian restaurants, usually listed clearly on the menu and receipt. The word comes from *coprire*, meaning "to cover," and originally referred to the cost of preparing the table, tablecloth, cutlery, and bread. Today, it represents a modest fee, typically ranging from €1 to €3 per person, though in tourist areas or more upscale establishments, it can be higher. While it might surprise visitors, the ***coperto*** is a deeply rooted Italian custom and an integral part of the dining experience. Importantly, the ***coperto*** is not an optional tip, which are not typical in Italy. The ***coperto*** is applied to everyone at the table, regardless of what or how much they order, and helps cover the restaurant's overhead costs, such as fresh bread, oil, and the welcoming table setting that make dining in Italy feel special. You might see a note on the menu saying, "*Pane e **coperto*** €2," which means "Bread and cover charge €2." This practice dates back to medieval times, when travelers paid for the right to sit at an inn's table and eat their own food under shelter. Over the centuries, it evolved into the modern ***coperto***. Rather than an inconvenience, it's seen as part of the experience, a small contribution to the care and comfort that define Italian dining.

Cornetto NOUN

(kor-NET-toh)

Italian croissant

A ***cornetto*** is a beloved Italian pastry that forms the heart of the traditional Italian breakfast. Similar in shape to the French croissant but distinct in flavor and texture, the ***cornetto*** is typically softer, slightly sweeter, and often filled with delicious ingredients like jam (in Italian, *marmellata*), custard (*crema*), or chocolate (*cioccolato*). A plain version, known as ***cornetto*** *vuoto*, is also popular and lightly dusted with powdered sugar. The name ***cornetto*** means "little horn," referring to its crescent shape. In cafés across Italy, mornings begin with the comforting pairing of *un* ***cornetto*** *e un cappuccino*, a ritual that defines the Italian breakfast. Unlike the hurried grab-and-go breakfasts common elsewhere, enjoying a ***cornetto*** is a moment of calm and connection. Italians often eat it while standing at the bar counter, chatting with the barista, or they may pair it with reading the newspaper. There are regional variations too: in northern Italy, the ***cornetto*** tends to be lighter and flakier, while in the south, it is denser and more fragrant, sometimes made with honey or orange zest. The ***cornetto*** reflects Italy's appreciation for craftsmanship and balance; it's indulgent but never heavy. Beyond being a pastry, the ***cornetto*** symbolizes Italian mornings and those few quiet minutes you can sit back and enjoy life before the day begins.

A Regional Rename In northern Italy, *brioche* is the common name for what elsewhere is called ***cornetto***. Same pastry, different regional word.

Cotechino con lenticchie NOUN PHRASE

(koh-teh-KEE-noh kon len-TEEK-kyeh)

Pork sausage with lentils

Cotechino con lenticchie is a traditional Italian dish eaten on New Year's Eve. It pairs *cotechino*, a large, richly seasoned pork sausage, with *lenticchie* (in English, "lentils"). Slow-cooked until tender, *cotechino* releases savory flavors that blend with the lentils, creating a comforting meal that embodies Italian celebration and tradition. This dish has its origins in northern Italy, particularly in Emilia-Romagna, a region famous for its charcuterie. The *cotechino* is made from pork, rind, and spices, encased and simmered for several hours until the meat becomes soft and full of flavor. It's typically sliced and served over the stewed lentils, sometimes accompanied by mashed potatoes or polenta. The result is a rich combination of textures and flavors: silky lentils, hearty sausage, and spices, which perfectly suits the winter season. ***Cotechino con lenticchie*** carries a deep cultural meaning. Eating lentils at midnight on *Capodanno* (New Year's Eve) is thought to ensure financial fortune because of their coin-like shape, while pork, a symbol of progress and abundance, represents moving forward into the new year with optimism. The meal is often enjoyed with a glass of wine as fireworks light up the night. More than a simple dish, ***cotechino con lenticchie*** is a ritual of hope and renewal in the year to come.

Cotto a puntino PHRASE

(KOHt-toh ah poon-TEE-noh)

Cooked to perfection

Cotto a puntino is an elegant Italian expression meaning "cooked to perfection" or "done just right." It's used to describe food that is neither undercooked nor overdone, but instead perfectly balanced in texture, flavor, and tenderness. The phrase reflects the precision that defines Italian cooking, where achieving ***cotto a puntino*** is a mark of culinary skill. Literally, *cotto* means "cooked," and *a puntino* comes from *punto* ("point"), suggesting something done to the precise point of perfection. You'll often hear it used in reference to meat, particularly steak. For example, *La bistecca è cotta a puntino* means "The steak is cooked perfectly." In this case, the adjective *cotto* changes to its feminine form *cotta* because it refers to the feminine noun *bistecca*. However, ***cotto a puntino*** isn't limited to meat. It can describe pasta, vegetables, or desserts baked to just the right consistency. For instance, *La pasta è cotta a puntino* means "The pasta is perfectly cooked."

When It Isn't *Cotto a Puntino* When food is *scotto*, it means it's been cooked too long, overdone, or overly soft. For example, *La pasta è scotta* means "The pasta is overcooked." It's the opposite of ***cotto a puntino***, and describes food that's lost its ideal texture or flavor. In Italy, calling pasta *scotta* is almost a culinary sin.

Dieta mediterranea NOUN PHRASE

(dee-EH-tah meh-dee-tehr-RAH-neh-ah)

Mediterranean diet

Dieta mediterranea refers to the traditional way of eating in countries bordering the Mediterranean Sea, particularly Italy, Greece, and southern Spain. It celebrates balance, moderation, and the use of fresh, local ingredients. Central to the ***dieta mediterranea*** are vegetables, fruits, whole grains, legumes, olive oil, nuts, and fish, with limited amounts of red meat and refined sugar. Meals are often accompanied by a glass of wine, enjoyed in moderation and as part of a relaxed, social experience. This diet is not just a set of nutritional guidelines; it's a lifestyle rooted in culture and community. In Italy, ***dieta mediterranea*** reflects a deep respect for seasonal produce and home-cooked meals shared with family. Olive oil, often called "liquid gold," is its cornerstone, providing healthy monounsaturated fats and rich flavor. Fish and legumes serve as the main protein sources. Scientifically, the ***dieta mediterranea*** is recognized as one of the healthiest diets in the world. Rich in antioxidants, fiber, and healthy fats, it supports heart health, reduces inflammation, and may increase longevity. In 2013, UNESCO even listed it as an Intangible Cultural Heritage of Humanity, acknowledging its role in promoting well-being and social connection. Ultimately, the ***dieta mediterranea*** embodies the Mediterranean way of life: balanced, joyful, and centered on good food and good company. It teaches that health comes not from restriction, but from mindful eating and natural ingredients.

Digestivo NOUN

(dee-jeh-STEE-voh)

Digestive drink

In the dining context, ***digestivo*** is a traditional Italian alcoholic beverage enjoyed after a meal, believed to help with digestion and bring the dining experience to a satisfying close. The word ***digestivo*** comes from *digerire*, meaning "to digest." Common *digestivi* (plural form) include *amaro* (a bitter herbal liqueur), *grappa* (a strong spirit made from grape pomace), and *limoncello* (a sweet lemon liqueur from southern Italy). Each offers a distinct flavor profile: *amaro* is earthy and complex, *grappa* is aromatic, and *limoncello* is bright and refreshing. These are regional variations: Veneto is famous for *grappa*, Campania for *limoncello*, and Tuscany for *amaro toscano*, each representing local traditions and ingredients. The ***digestivo*** usually follows the *caffè* at the end of the meal and is sipped slowly, often in small and cold glasses. It's not about indulgence but about closure, a symbolic way of saying the meal, and the company, are complete. Italians might offer you ***digestivo*** at home after a Sunday lunch or order it in a restaurant as a finale.

After Dinner, Italian Style One of the most beloved *digestivi* is *limoncello*, a bright, sweet liqueur made from the zest of lemons. It originates from the Amalfi Coast and the island of Capri, where lemons such as the Sfusato Amalfitano (on the Amalfi Coast) and the Femminello (on Capri) grow. Traditionally, *limoncello* is homemade, steeping lemon peels in pure alcohol before mixing with sugar and water.

Essere una buona forchetta IDIOMATIC EXPRESSION

(ES-seh-reh oo-nah BWOH-nah for-KET-tah)

To be a good eater

Essere una buona forchetta literally means "to be a good fork," but is used to describe someone who loves eating and truly appreciates good food. The expression is lighthearted, often used to compliment those who enjoy mealtimes. When you say someone is *una buona forchetta*, you're not just calling them a big eater; you're recognizing their joyful relationship with food and their willingness to try new dishes. For example, you might say, "*Mia nonna è una buona forchetta!*" meaning "My grandmother is a good eater!" implying she enjoys every bite. The main verb *essere* ("to be") is conjugated to match the subject, so when talking about *nonna*, the verb *essere* changes to *è* ("is"). The phrase ***essere una buona forchetta*** can be used humorously among friends or within families, celebrating the Italian love of food as an important part of life. Ultimately, ***essere una buona forchetta*** captures the Italian philosophy of living fully through food.

Don't Skip the Sound The word *forchetta* is pronounced with the stress on the second syllable. The "ch" combination in Italian makes a hard *k* sound, as in "cat." Make sure to roll the *r* slightly, as Italian words do. The double *t* is held a bit longer than a single *t*, giving it a longer sound.

Fare il bis PHRASE

(FAH-reh eel BEES)

To have seconds

Fare il bis is a common Italian expression that refers to enjoying a second helping of food. The phrase comes from the world of music and theater, where *bis* means "encore," a repeat performance requested by an enthusiastic audience. In the context of food, it carries the same joyful spirit: when a dish is so delicious that you simply must have more. For example, at a family dinner, someone might say, "*Faccio il bis della pasta!*" meaning "I'm having seconds of the pasta!" Here the verb *fare* is conjugated to match the subject "I." ***Fare il bis*** is a friendly, lighthearted way to express appreciation for the meal. In Italian homes, hearing ***fare il bis*** at the table is considered one of the highest compliments. It means the food was so good it deserves a repeat performance. This phrase also reflects the Italian philosophy of eating as a social experience. Meals are not rushed but shared and celebrated. ***Fare il bis*** captures that Italian love for good food and good company, because when something is truly *buono* ("good"), one helping is simply not enough.

Beyond Seconds When eating, *fare il tris* is used informally to mean having three portions of dishes: *Ho fatto il tris di primi* ("I had three different first courses").

Fare la scarpetta IDIOMATIC EXPRESSION

(FAH-reh lah skar-PEHT-tah)

To mop up with bread

Fare la scarpetta is one of the most endearing Italian expressions, meaning "to mop up with bread." It refers to the act of using a small piece of bread to scoop up the last traces of sauce left on a plate, often after pasta, stew, or roast dishes. Grammatically, *scarpetta* is a feminine singular noun, derived from *scarpa* (translating to "shoe"). It uses the diminutive suffix *-etta*, which conveys smallness and affection. Though its exact origin is uncertain, many believe *scarpetta* describes how the bread "walks" across the plate to collect every last drop of flavor. This simple gesture embodies the refusal to let any bit of good food go to waste. ***Fare la scarpetta*** is a sign that the dish was too good to leave behind. In Italy you might hear, "*Faccio la scarpetta!*" ("I'm mopping up with bread!") when dining out. While ***fare la scarpetta*** is acceptable and even encouraged in informal settings, it's considered slightly impolite in formal dining contexts. In elegant restaurants or official dinners, where table manners are expected to be more refined, wiping the plate with bread might appear too casual. Historically, such behavior was seen as something done at home, not in front of company. Overall, more than just a table habit, ***fare la scarpetta*** reflects the idea that food is not only nourishment but also appreciation.

Fiorentina NOUN

(fee-or-en-TEE-nah)

Florentine steak

Fiorentina, short for *bistecca alla* ***fiorentina***, is one of the most iconic dishes of Tuscan cuisine. It's a large, thick-cut porterhouse or T-bone steak traditionally made from Chianina cattle, one of Italy's oldest and most prized breeds. The meat is known for its tenderness and deep flavor. True to Tuscan simplicity, the ***fiorentina*** is seasoned only with salt, freshly ground black pepper, and a drizzle of extra-virgin olive oil, allowing the rich taste of the beef to shine through. The steak is cooked over a wood or charcoal fire, grilled quickly on both sides to achieve a flavorful crust while keeping the inside rare or medium-rare. In fact, cooking it beyond that is considered a culinary offense in Tuscany, as it would lose its juiciness and texture. A proper *bistecca alla* ***fiorentina*** is typically cut at least 3 to 4 centimeters (up to 1.5 inches) thick and weighs around 1 to 1.5 kilograms (2.25–3.25 pounds), making it a dish meant to be shared between two or more people. This legendary steak has its origins in Florence, where it has been enjoyed for centuries. Today, it remains a symbol of Tuscan pride and hospitality, served in traditional *trattorie* and upscale restaurants. Eating *una* ***fiorentina*** is more than enjoying a steak; it's a celebration of quality.

Focaccia NOUN

(foh-KAH-cchah)

Flatbread

Focaccia is a beloved Italian flatbread known for its soft, airy interior and slightly crispy crust. The name derives from the Latin *focus*, meaning "fireplace," as the bread was originally baked over the fire or on hot coals. Made from a simple dough of flour, water, yeast, salt, and olive oil, ***focaccia*** is often topped with rosemary, coarse salt, and a drizzle of extra-virgin olive oil before being baked. You can enjoy ***focaccia*** in countless ways: as an appetizer, a side dish, a quick snack, or even the base for sandwiches. Regional variations abound: ***focaccia*** *genovese* from Liguria is thin and oily with a delicate crunch, while ***focaccia*** *barese* from Puglia incorporates cherry tomatoes, olives, and potatoes in the dough for extra flavor. In Tuscany, *schiacciata* is the local version, slightly saltier and often served plain or split open and filled with cheese or prosciutto. The charm of ***focaccia*** lies in its simplicity and versatility. Whether enjoyed warm from the oven, dipped in olive oil, or paired with a glass of wine, ***focaccia*** captures the spirit of Italian comfort food. This versatility makes it a favorite across the country, from family kitchens to street bakeries, where it's sold by the slice and eaten on the go. In every bite of ***focaccia***, there's a taste of Italy's love for simple, shared pleasures.

Fritto misto NOUN PHRASE

(FREET-toh MEES-toh)

Mixed fried food

Fritto misto literally means "mixed fry" and refers to an assortment of foods, most often seafood or vegetables, lightly coated in flour or batter and deep-fried until golden and crispy. The name captures the spirit of the dish: a mix of textures and flavors that come together in one crunchy plate. Common ingredients include shrimp, squid, small fish, zucchini, and artichokes, though the combination varies from region to region. Along the Ligurian and Venetian coasts, ***fritto misto*** *di mare* ("mixed fried seafood") reigns supreme with freshly caught fish, served with lemon wedges. In northern and central Italy, ***fritto misto*** may include vegetables, offering a hearty and rustic variation. The secret to great ***fritto misto*** lies in the lightness of its coating and the temperature of the oil: hot enough to crisp the outside while keeping the inside tender. Italians take pride in achieving the perfect balance, never excessively greasy, always crisp and airy. Traditionally served as a shared appetizer or a casual main dish, ***fritto misto*** embodies the Italian love for hands-on eating. A squeeze of lemon and a pinch of salt are often all that's needed to enhance its natural goodness. ***Fritto misto*** can be enjoyed seaside with a glass of white wine or at home for a simple yet exciting meal.

Gelato NOUN, ADJECTIVE

(jeh-LAH-toh)

Ice cream

Gelato is Italy's world-famous version of ice cream, celebrated for its creamy and vibrant flavor. As an adjective, the word simply means "frozen" in Italian. Unlike traditional ice cream, ***gelato*** contains less fat and less air, which gives it a denser consistency and a more intense taste. Made with fresh, high-quality ingredients such as milk, sugar, eggs, and natural flavorings, ***gelato*** showcases Italy's devotion to simplicity and flavor. Another key difference is temperature: ***Gelato*** is served slightly warmer than ice cream, allowing its texture to remain. The result is a dessert that feels lighter and more satisfying. Common flavors include *pistacchio* ("pistachio"), *nocciola* ("hazelnut"), *stracciatella* ("chocolate shavings"), and *limone* ("lemon"), though modern *gelaterie* ("ice cream shops") also offer creative combinations like *caramello salato* ("salted caramel") or *fichi e noci* ("figs and walnuts"). Enjoying ***gelato*** in Italy is a common ritual. Italians often take an evening stroll, known as *passeggiata*, with a ***gelato*** in hand. ***Gelato*** is typically served in either a *cono* ("cone") or a *coppetta* ("small cup"). Choosing a *cono* adds a crunchy, edible touch, while a *coppetta* lets you enjoy it more slowly with a small spoon. Both options often allow for two or more flavors, making every ***gelato*** experience customizable.

Liscio come l'olio IDIOMATIC EXPRESSION

(LEE-shoh KOH-meh LOH-lyoh)

Smooth sailing

Liscio come l'olio is a charming Italian idiom that literally means "as smooth as oil." It is used to describe something that goes effortlessly well, much like the way extra-virgin olive oil, one of Italy's most treasured culinary staples, glides without resistance. In a country where olive oil is as fundamental to cooking as salt, it is no surprise that Italians reached for it to describe life's seamless moments. You might hear someone say, "*È andato tutto **liscio come l'olio***" ("Everything went smoothly") after a dinner party runs perfectly, a recipe comes together without effort, or an event unfolds without a hitch. In conversation, the expression carries a tone of warm satisfaction and relief. Beyond the kitchen, olive oil holds deep cultural symbolism in Italy, representing richness and good fortune, so comparing something to it adds a sense of positivity and grace that goes far beyond mere smoothness.

Speaking of Opposites An opposite expression to ***liscio come l'olio*** is *andare storto*, meaning "to go wrong." Literally, *storto* means "crooked," the opposite of smooth or straight. For example, *Tutto è andato storto!* means "Everything went wrong!" You may hear it being used when plans fail, situations become complicated, or things don't go as expected. While ***liscio come l'olio*** celebrates ease, *andare storto* is a reminder that not everything in life flows perfectly.

Merenda NOUN

(meh-REN-dah)

Afternoon snack

Merenda is a light snack enjoyed in the late afternoon, usually between *pranzo* ("lunch") and *cena* ("dinner"). In Italy, it's more than just a small bite, it's a pause in the day, especially loved by children after school. Typical *merende* (plural form) include a piece of fruit, a slice of bread with jam or Nutella, a pastry, or even a small slice of pizza or *focaccia*. The goal isn't indulgence but balance: enough to satisfy hunger without spoiling dinner. The word ***merenda*** comes from the Latin *merēre*, meaning "to deserve" or "something to be earned," the idea of a reward after work or study. ***Merenda*** is usually not rushed or eaten on the go; it's a time to sit, relax, and enjoy something simple and also satisfying. While often associated with children, adults also take part in this tradition, especially in regions where the afternoon is slow-paced and social life centers around cafés and bakeries. In northern Italy, people might enjoy a small pastry with coffee; in the south, a refreshing granita or a piece of seasonal fruit. The ***merenda*** reminds Italians that eating isn't only about nourishment: It's also about slowing down, taking a break, and finding joy in small everyday moments.

A Late-Night Bite ***Spuntino di mezzanotte*** **means "midnight snack," usually something small and informal eaten late at night. It's lighter than a meal and often spontaneous:** ***Dopo il film abbiamo fatto uno spuntino di mezzanotte*** **("After the movie we had a midnight snack").**

Mozzarella di bufala NOUN PHRASE

(moht-tsah-REHL-lah dee BOO-fah-lah)

Buffalo mozzarella

Mozzarella di bufala is a creamy Italian cheese made from the milk of water buffalo, primarily raised in the regions of Campania and Lazio. This cheese is richer, softer, and more flavorful than regular cow's milk mozzarella (*fior di latte*), with a smooth, elastic texture and a subtle tang that reflects the quality of the buffalo milk. The result is a cheese that offers a perfect balance of sweetness, saltiness, and creaminess. Traditionally produced near Naples, ***Mozzarella di Bufala*** *Campana DOP* is protected by a designation of origin, ensuring it's made according to time-honored methods and with milk from local herds. The process begins with fresh buffalo milk that's curdled, stretched, and shaped by hand into white orbs. The cheese is stored in light brine to preserve its softness and flavor. Best enjoyed fresh, ***mozzarella di bufala*** is often served at room temperature to bring out its natural creaminess. It goes well in simple dishes that highlight its flavor, such as *insalata caprese* ("caprese salad"), where slices of mozzarella are layered with ripe tomatoes, basil, olive oil, and a sprinkle of sea salt. You can also pair it with grilled vegetables, cured meats, or fresh bread. Beyond its culinary uses, ***mozzarella di bufala*** represents the heart of southern Italian food culture: respect for local ingredients and the joy of simplicity.

Orecchiette NOUN

(oh-rehk-KYEHT-teh)

Small, ear-shaped pasta

Orecchiette, meaning "little ears," are a traditional pasta from the southern Italian region of Puglia, particularly the city of Bari. Their name comes from *orecchio* ("ear") combined with the diminutive suffix *-ette*, which emphasizes their small, rounded form. Each piece of ***orecchiette*** resembles a tiny ear, concave and slightly rough on the surface, perfect for catching and holding sauces. Made simply from semolina flour and water, ***orecchiette*** embody the rustic, homemade essence of Apulian (Puglia) cuisine. Traditionally, women would sit together outdoors in the afternoons, rolling and shaping each piece by hand with a knife or thumb. This image of shared craftsmanship remains one of the most charming scenes in southern Italy's culinary tradition. The most iconic dish featuring this pasta is ***orecchiette*** *alle cime di rapa*, a regional specialty made with turnip tops, garlic, anchovies, and chili, creating a blend of bitterness, saltiness, and spice. However, ***orecchiette*** also pair beautifully with tomato sauces, sausage, broccoli, or fresh ricotta. Their texture makes them one of Italy's most versatile and comforting pastas. Beyond their taste, ***orecchiette*** represent how simple ingredients, combined with care and tradition, can create something extraordinary. Made by hand at home or enjoyed in a rustic *trattoria* ("traditional restaurant"), ***orecchiette*** carry the warmth, authenticity, and soul of southern Italian cooking. Each "little ear" is a delicious tribute to centuries of culinary heritage.

Pasta al dente NOUN PHRASE

(PAH-stah al DEN-teh)

Pasta firm to the bite

Pasta al dente is one of the cornerstones of Italian cooking. Literally meaning "pasta to the tooth," *al dente* describes pasta that is cooked until it offers a slight resistance when bitten. It should be tender yet firm, never soft or mushy. Achieving this texture requires attention and timing, as even a minute too long in boiling water can turn perfectly *al dente* pasta into something *scotto* ("overcooked"). Cooking ***pasta al dente*** enhances not only texture but also flavor. The firmer bite allows the pasta to better absorb and hold onto sauces. Italians view ***pasta al dente*** as a mark of skill and care in the kitchen. In fact, many pasta packages in Italy include specific *al dente* cooking times, underscoring its importance. Beyond its literal meaning, *al dente* has become a metaphor for the Italian way of life: balanced, lively, and never overdone. Just as perfectly cooked pasta maintains its shape and character, Italians value a life that's full of texture and energy, not rushed or softened by excess.

Pasta, the Italian Way Before adding pasta to the boiling water, Italians always salt the water generously, often saying it should be *salata come il mare* ("as salty as the sea"). The salt enhances the pasta's flavor from within, not just the sauce added later. It's a simple but essential step that will transform your plain pasta into a perfectly seasoned foundation for any dish.

Piadina NOUN

(pyah-DEE-nah)

Thin flatbread

A ***piadina*** is a thin, soft flatbread that originates from the Emilia-Romagna region of northern Italy. Traditionally made with simply flour, lard (or olive oil), salt, and water, it's cooked on a hot griddle known as a *testo*. The result is a warm, slightly chewy bread with a hint of crispness around the edges. Humble in origin but quite versatile, ***piadina*** has been a staple of Italian street food and home cooking for centuries. Its roots date back to ancient times, when it was baked on clay discs over open fires, serving as an everyday bread for farmers and travelers. Today, this rustic bread has evolved into one of Italy's most beloved snacks. A classic ***piadina*** is often filled with *prosciutto crudo* ("raw cured ham"), *squacquerone* cheese, and fresh arugula, though modern versions include countless variations, from vegetarian to sweet, including Nutella. Folded in half and eaten by hand, ***piadina*** is perfect for lunch, picnics, or a quick bite on the go. Small shops called *piadinerie* specialize in serving freshly made *piadine* (plural form), and you'll find them all over Italy, from beach towns on the Adriatic coast to small city centers.

Pizza bianca NOUN PHRASE

(PEET-tsah BYAN-kah)

White pizza

Pizza bianca, meaning "white pizza," is a Roman specialty that celebrates simplicity and flavor. Unlike traditional pizza topped with tomato sauce, ***pizza bianca*** is made with just a drizzle of olive oil, a sprinkle of salt, and sometimes fresh rosemary. The result is a pizza with a crisp exterior and soft, airy interior. Despite its name, it's not always eaten like pizza. It's more like a flatbread, often baked in long rectangular trays and sliced into pieces at bakeries throughout Rome. Its origins are humble. In ancient Roman bakeries, ***pizza bianca*** began as a way to test the oven's temperature before baking the daily bread. Bakers would flatten a small piece of dough, season it lightly, and slide it into the oven to gauge the heat. Over time, this "test dough" became so delicious that it turned into a tradition of its own. Today, Romans enjoy ***pizza bianca*** throughout the day, especially midmorning, eaten warm and topped with slices of *prosciutto crudo* or *mortadella*. It's sold by weight in local bakeries (*forni*) and is considered the ultimate street food. The word *bianca* ("white") highlights its minimalism, but don't let its simplicity fool you. When made well, ***pizza bianca*** embodies everything Italians cherish about food: quality ingredients and the beauty of doing something simple exceptionally well.

Polenta NOUN

(poh-LEN-tah)

Cornmeal dish

Polenta is one of Italy's oldest and most comforting dishes, a golden porridge made from coarsely ground cornmeal. Its roots stretch back to ancient times, long before corn arrived in Europe. The word ***polenta*** comes from the Latin *pollen*, meaning "fine flour" and early versions were made with grains like millet, barley, or spelt. When corn was introduced from the Americas in the late fifteenth century, northern Italians quickly adopted it, creating the corn-based ***polenta*** popular today. Originally considered the food of farmers and peasants, ***polenta*** was loved for its affordability and ability to nourish large families. Over time, it evolved into a dish celebrated across Italy, particularly in the Alpine and northern regions such as Lombardy, Veneto, and Trentino, where it remains a symbol of home cooking. Traditionally, ***polenta*** is slowly cooked in a copper pot (*paiolo*), stirred patiently for nearly an hour until it becomes thick, creamy, and smooth. You can be served ***polenta*** soft and warm, topped with stews, melted cheese, mushrooms, or sausage, or cooled and sliced to be grilled, baked, or fried. In mountain villages, it's often the centerpiece of a meal, shared straight from the pot at the family table.

A Mountain Specialty A traditional dish from northern Italy, especially Bergamo and Valtellina, ***polenta*** *taragna* is made with buckwheat flour and enriched with butter and melted cheeses like Bitto or Branzi. It's darker, richer, and more rustic than classic yellow ***polenta***.

Pranzo domenicale NOUN PHRASE

(PRAN-tsoh doh-meh-nee-KAH-leh)

Sunday lunch

Pranzo domenicale, or "Sunday lunch," is one of the most cherished Italian traditions, a weekly ritual that goes beyond just eating. It's a time for family, connection, and celebration, when generations gather around the table to share food. The phrase combines *pranzo* ("lunch") with *domenicale* ("of Sunday"), encapsulating the rhythm of Italian life: work during the week, rest and be together on Sunday. Typically, the ***pranzo domenicale*** is a grand meal made up of multiple courses. It begins with *antipasti*, perhaps cured meats, cheeses, or *crostini*, followed by a rich *primo* ("first course") such as lasagna, risotto, or fresh pasta. The *secondo* ("second course") might feature roasted meats or fish, accompanied by *contorni* ("side dishes") like potatoes or seasonal vegetables. Dessert, or *dolce*, often includes homemade treats like *crostata* or *tiramisù*, finishing with fruit, espresso, and maybe a *digestivo* ("digestive drink") to close the meal. This tradition is rooted in Italy's agricultural history, when Sunday was the one day families could rest after a week of labor. It became a moment to reconnect and give thanks for abundance. Even today, in modern cities, the spirit of ***pranzo domenicale*** continues with restaurants filled with families. More than a meal, ***pranzo domenicale*** represents the Italian philosophy of *convivialità*, that is, the joy of eating together.

Risotto NOUN

(ree-ZOHT-toh)

Creamy rice dish

Risotto is one of the great symbols of northern Italian cuisine, a dish that transforms simple rice into something rich and comforting. Made by slowly cooking rice in broth while stirring constantly, ***risotto*** achieves its signature creaminess through technique rather than added cream. The starch released from the grains creates a velvety texture that defines the dish. The word ***risotto*** comes from *riso* ("rice"), and its history stretches back to the Renaissance, when rice cultivation spread through Lombardy and Piedmont. The most famous version, ***risotto*** *alla milanese* ("risotto Milan-style"), is rumored to date from the 1500s and is flavored with *zafferano* (translating to "saffron"), which gives it a golden color and delicate aroma. Other beloved varieties include ***risotto*** *ai funghi* ("mushroom risotto"), ***risotto*** *ai frutti di mare* ("seafood risotto"), and ***risotto*** *al Barolo* (made with red wine from Piedmont). Each region adapts the dish according to local ingredients, but all share the same principle: patience and care. Traditionally, ***risotto*** is made with short-grain rice varieties like Arborio or Carnaroli. The process invites you to slow down, toasting the rice (*tostatura*) and adding wine before gradually incorporating the warm broth and stirring until the texture becomes perfectly creamy. Beyond its technique, ***risotto*** embodies the Italian culinary philosophy that simplicity and time create beauty. It's not a dish to rush. ***Risotto*** asks for attention, rhythm, and love.

Salute NOUN, INTERJECTION

(sah-LOO-teh)

Health; Cheers

Salute is a small word with big meaning in Italian culture, used both to refer to health and as a celebratory toast. Derived from the Latin *salus*, meaning "health," "safety," or "well-being," the term reflects how interconnected food, drink, and wellness are in Italian. When Italians raise a glass and say "***Salute!***" they are not simply saying "cheers," but wishing good health and prosperity to everyone present. ***Salute*** is also used in everyday conversation to refer to physical health. Asking "*Com'è la tua **salute**?*" ("How's your health?") is a genuine inquiry, not a formality. In meals, especially long ones, the Italian toast "*Alla **salute**!*" ("To health!") marks the beginning of a shared experience, reinforcing bonds at the table. Unlike more casual toasts elsewhere, Italians tend to make eye contact when saying ***salute***, as a sign of respect and sincerity. The word appears frequently in Italian expressions, such as *Alla tua **salute*** ("To your health") or *Essere in buona **salute*** ("To be in good health").

A Cultural Gesture In Italy, failing to make eye contact while saying ***salute*** during a toast is sometimes considered bad manners, as the toast symbolizes mutual respect and shared good fortune.

Spaghettata NOUN

(spah-GEHT-tah-tah)

Informal spaghetti meal

Spaghettata refers to an informal, often spontaneous gathering centered around a simple plate of spaghetti. More than a specific recipe, it describes a social moment, typically late at night or after an event, when friends come together to eat pasta and talk. The dish itself is usually very simple and this simplicity is intentional, reflecting the idea that good company matters more than elaborate cooking. The word comes directly from *spaghetti*, Italy's most iconic pasta, and the suffix *-ata*, which implies an event or collective experience. *Spaghettate* (plural form) are rooted in Italian culture, and they are unplanned, relaxed, and joyful, often accompanied by laughter, wine, and music. There is no rigid structure, no formal table setting, and no strict schedule. What defines a ***spaghettata*** is the spirit of sharing and improvisation. In Italian cinema and literature, *spaghettate* often symbolize friendship and human connection. In this way, the ***spaghettata*** perfectly expresses the Italian belief that even the simplest food, when shared, can become memorable.

Late-Night Tradition *Spaghettate* are especially popular during summer holidays and seaside trips, when groups gather late at night after concerts, festivals, or beach outings.

Tartufo NOUN

(tar-TOO-foh)

Truffle

Tartufo is the Italian word for "truffle," one of the most prized and aromatic ingredients in Italian cuisine. These rare fungi grow underground, and you can typically find them near the roots of oak, hazelnut, or poplar trees. Traditionally, trained dogs, called *cani da* ***tartufo***, are used to locate them by scent. The word ***tartufo*** comes from the Latin *terrae tūber*, meaning "swelling" or "lump," referring to its rounded shape. Italy is home to some of the world's most celebrated truffles, particularly the white truffle of Alba in Piedmont and the black truffles found in Umbria and Tuscany. White truffles are especially valuable and are usually eaten raw, shaved thinly over dishes like pasta, risotto, or eggs, allowing their intense aroma to shine. Black truffles, slightly more robust, can be cooked and are often used in sauces, butters, and fillings. ***Tartufo*** is associated with luxury, considering its premium price, and regional pride. Entire festivals, such as the *Fiera del* ***Tartufo*** *Bianco d'Alba*, celebrate the harvest of truffles each autumn.

> **Seasonal Treasure** White truffles are only available for a few months each year, typically from October to December, making them a symbol of autumn in northern Italy.

Tiramisù NOUN

(tee-rah-mee-SOO)

Coffee-flavored dessert

Tiramisù is one of Italy's most beloved desserts, known worldwide for its creamy texture and coffee flavor. The name literally means "pick me up" or "lift me up," referring to the energizing combination of espresso and cocoa. Though its exact origins are debated, ***tiramisù*** is generally associated with the Veneto and Friuli-Venezia Giulia regions and is thought to have emerged in the mid-twentieth century. Traditional ***tiramisù*** is made by layering *savoiardi* ("ladyfinger cookies") soaked in espresso with a smooth cream of mascarpone cheese, raw eggs, and sugar, then finished with a dusting of cocoa powder. Unlike many desserts, it is not baked, relying instead on chilling to set its structure. ***Tiramisù*** is often served at the end of family meals, celebrations, and special occasions, though it is also commonly found in *trattorie* and bakeries. Its popularity lies in its balance: sweet but not overwhelming. Over time, countless variations have emerged, including versions with chocolate, berries, or liqueurs, though many Italians insist on the classic recipe. ***Tiramisù*** reflects Italian culinary values of simplicity, quality ingredients, and comfort. When you're pronouncing ***tiramisù***, pay particular attention to stressing the final vowel that is accented.

A Modern Classic The iconic ***tiramisù*** is one of the few Italian dishes that became popular relatively recently, yet it feels timeless and traditional.

Tortellini in brodo NOUN PHRASE

(tor-tehl-LEE-nee een BROH-doh)

Stuffed pasta in broth

Tortellini in brodo is a classic dish from the Emilia-Romagna region, especially associated with Bologna and Modena. It consists of small, ring-shaped stuffed pasta served in a clear, flavorful meat broth, *brodo* in Italian. The filling traditionally includes pork, *prosciutto, mortadella, parmigiano* ("parmesan"), and nutmeg. According to legend, the shape of *tortellini* was inspired by the goddess Venus's navel. That said, the story has several versions, with Modena claiming the muse was instead the Renaissance beauty, Lucrezia Borgia. ***Tortellini in brodo*** is most closely associated with winter and festive occasions, particularly Christmas. For many Italian families, it is the centerpiece of holiday meals, symbolizing comfort and tradition. Unlike heavier pasta dishes, ***tortellini in brodo*** is delicate and balanced, allowing each component to shine. It reflects the culinary refinement of Emilia-Romagna, a region famous for its rich gastronomy. More than just food, this dish represents family heritage, as recipes are often passed down through generations.

The Small Things In Italian, adding *-ino* to the end of a word creates a diminutive, meaning something smaller or more delicate. For example, *tortello* becomes *tortellino*: a smaller, ring-shaped stuffed pasta. The plural form of *tortellino* is *tortellini*. On the other hand, to make something bigger or more impressive, you can use the suffix *-one*. For example, *tortello* becomes *tortellone*: a much larger stuffed pasta.

Trattoria NOUN

(traht-toh-REE-ah)

Traditional restaurant

A ***trattoria*** is a traditional Italian restaurant known for its relaxed atmosphere, home-style cooking, and local specialties. Less formal than a *ristorante*, *trattorie* (plural form) are often family-run and rooted in their communities. Menus in *trattorie* are usually limited and seasonal, changing according to available ingredients and regional traditions. Dishes are hearty and straightforward, often based on recipes passed down through generations. Prices are typically more affordable, making *trattorie* accessible places for locals. Historically, *trattorie* served workers, travelers, and neighbors. Today, they remain symbols of authenticity and culinary identity. Eating in a ***trattoria*** is usually not about trends or presentation, but about flavor, tradition, and hospitality. *Trattorie* can offer you the most genuine taste of Italian cuisine and everyday life.

Where Is the Menu? Many *trattorie* do not offer written menus; instead, the staff lists the dishes verbally based on what is freshest and available that day. This means the menu can change daily, depending on the season and the quality of ingredients. Ordering this way is very traditional and reflects a kitchen that cooks according to freshness and what is available rather than a fixed menu.

Trofie al pesto NOUN PHRASE

(TROH-fee al PES-toh)

Pasta with basil pesto

Trofie al pesto is a quintessential dish from Liguria, particularly the area around Genoa. *Trofie* are short, twisted pasta made from durum wheat and water, designed to hold sauce. *Pesto alla genovese*, which is "pesto Genovese-style," is made from fresh basil, pine nuts, garlic, *Parmigiano-Reggiano*, *pecorino*, olive oil, and salt. The combination reflects the Liguria region's geography: herbs, olive groves, and simplicity. ***Trofie al pesto*** can be served with boiled potatoes and green beans mixed directly into the pasta, creating a complete, balanced dish. The pesto sauce itself is never cooked; instead, it is gently tossed with the hot pasta to preserve its aroma and color. If *trofie* isn't available, the pesto sauce works best with any short or twisted pasta shapes that can hold the sauce well. Common alternatives include *fusilli* and *farfalle*. The key is choosing a pasta with enough texture or surface area to catch the pesto, rather than very smooth shapes.

Mortar Matters **Traditional pesto is made using a wooden or marble *mortaio* ("mortar") and pestle, which helps preserve the basil's delicate oils and aroma.**

Uovo di Pasqua NOUN PHRASE

(WOH-voh dee PAH-skwa)

Easter chocolate egg

The ***uovo di Pasqua*** is one of the most beloved and recognizable Italian Easter traditions. It consists of a large, hollow chocolate egg with a surprise hidden inside, turning Easter into a moment of anticipation. Unlike the small, individually wrapped Easter eggs you'd see in many other countries, Italian Easter eggs are often impressively large and wrapped in colorful, decorative foil, making them feel like a true gift. What makes the ***uovo di Pasqua*** especially special is the surprise inside. Each egg contains a small gift, and the excitement of breaking the chocolate open together is a key part of the experience, particularly for children. The surprise can be simple, like a small toy, or more meaningful, such as a necklace, depending on who the egg is for. *Uova di Pasqua* (plural) are exchanged not only among children but also between family members, friends, and romantic partners. Chocolate varieties range widely, from classic milk chocolate to white chocolate, dark chocolate, and even artisanal, high-quality versions that can be quite expensive. In recent years, gourmet and handcrafted eggs have become increasingly popular, especially among adults. For couples in Italy, exchanging Easter eggs with personalized surprises hidden inside makes the tradition both playful and intimate. Ultimately, the ***uovo di Pasqua*** is not just about chocolate, but about sharing a moment with loved ones.

Va a nozze con IDIOMATIC EXPRESSION

(vah ah NOT-tseh kon)

It goes perfectly with

Va a nozze con literally means "it goes to wedding with," but in Italian, it carries the figurative meaning of "it goes perfectly with" or "it is an ideal match." The phrase expresses harmony and the satisfaction that comes from a perfect pairing, much like the joy of two people uniting in marriage. Italians use it often when talking about food, flavors, or anything that combines seamlessly. For example, *Il vino bianco* ***va a nozze con*** *il pesce* means "White wine goes perfectly with fish," while *Il cioccolato* ***va a nozze con*** *le fragole* translates as "Chocolate goes perfectly with strawberries." The imagery of a wedding conveys the idea of balance and union: two distinct elements that come together to create something even greater. Grammatically, *va* means "it goes," *a nozze* means "to wedding," and *con*, "with," introduces what complements the subject. Though it originated in culinary contexts, the expression is also now used more broadly. You might hear someone say, "*Il blu* ***va a nozze con*** *il bianco*" (translating to "Blue goes perfectly with white") when describing colors, or "*La musica* ***va a nozze con*** *la poesia*" ("Music goes perfectly with poetry") to express artistic harmony. Ultimately, ***va a nozze con*** reflects the Italian love for the beauty found in balance. It celebrates the moments when things, whether tastes, colors, or ideas, fit so naturally that they seem destined to be together.

Vin brulé NOUN PHRASE

(veen broo-LEH)

Mulled wine

Vin brulé is the Italian version of mulled wine and a symbol of comfort, especially during the colder months and throughout the Christmas season. It is made by gently heating red wine with sugar and warm spices such as cinnamon and cloves, along with citrus peel and sometimes star anise. As it simmers, ***vin brulé*** releases a rich aroma that evokes winter holidays. The name ***vin brulé*** comes from the French *vin brûlé*, meaning "burnt wine," a reference to the heating process rather than actual burning. In fact, the wine is never boiled but warmed slowly to allow the flavors to blend without losing alcohol and depth. Each region and family may have its own variation, adjusting spices and sweetness to taste. ***Vin brulé*** is especially popular in northern Italy, particularly in Alpine and mountainous regions. It is a staple at Christmas markets, winter fairs, and outdoor festivals, where it is often served steaming hot in ceramic mugs that help retain warmth. More than just a drink, ***vin brulé*** brings people together during the cold season, making it a sensory and cultural hallmark of winter in Italy.

5

Family and Traditions

In Italy, family and traditions form the heart of everyday life. Relationships are nurtured through time spent together, shared rituals, and customs passed down from generation to generation. On a larger scale, shared traditions marking holidays and seasonal gatherings bring Italian people together as a whole. From celebrating a *battesimo* or *onomastico* to gathering for *settimana bianca*, this chapter guides you through the moments that strengthen family and community bonds and create a sense of belonging. In learning these words and expressions, you'll open a window into Italian values, where family and traditions come first, memories are cherished, and the past remains present in daily life.

Agriturismo NOUN

(ah-gree-too-REE-zmoh)

Rural restaurant; Farm stay

Agriturismo is a uniquely Italian concept that blends agriculture, hospitality, and family tradition. The word comes from *agricoltura* ("agriculture") and *turismo* ("tourism") and refers to working farms that welcome guests for meals, lodging, or both. The concept of ***agriturismo*** emerged in the late twentieth century as a way to support rural communities, preserve traditional farming practices, and protect the Italian countryside from abandonment. By law, these establishments must remain connected to agricultural activity, meaning the farm itself is central, not just decorative. What sets ***agriturismo*** apart is its deep connection to place and people. Meals are prepared using ingredients grown on the property or sourced locally, following seasonal rhythms. Guests can usually enjoy homemade pasta, fresh vegetables, olive oil, cheese, or wine produced on-site. Staying at an ***agriturismo*** offers immersion into rural life: waking to vineyard views, hearing farm animals, and experiencing the slower pace of the countryside. Many hosts share stories, recipes, and customs, turning a stay into a true cultural exchange. ***Agriturismo*** reflects core Italian values: respect for the land, pride in local food, and the belief that the best moments in life are shared around a table with the people you love.

Andrà tutto bene PHRASE

(ahn-DRAH TOOT-toh BEH-neh)

Everything will be alright

Andrà tutto bene is a phrase of reassurance that expresses hope, patience, and quiet strength. Literally meaning "will go everything well," it uses the verb *andare* ("to go") and looks forward rather than making guarantees. Italians often use it during moments of uncertainty, difficulty, or emotional vulnerability. This phrase became deeply tied to family and tradition during the early days of the COVID-19 pandemic in Italy, when families hung rainbow signs with this phrase from their windows as a symbol of hope and unity. ***Andrà tutto bene*** can be spoken to comfort a child, encourage a friend, or calm oneself in challenging times. Unlike stronger declarations of certainty, ***andrà tutto bene*** carries gentleness. It acknowledges that problems exist but chooses trust in the future. This reflects an Italian emotional approach to life: facing reality while maintaining optimism rooted in community and shared experience. You can use this phrase with gestures, a smile, or a reassuring tone, reinforcing its warmth. ***Andrà tutto bene*** reminds Italian people that life is a journey, and that hope, when shared, can be as powerful as action.

Say It Clearly ***Tutto*** **is pronounced** ***(TOOT-toh)*****. The double consonant** ***t*** **is held longer, the** ***u*** **is a clean "oo" sound, and the stress is on the first syllable.**

Battesimo NOUN

(baht-TEH-zee-moh)

Baptism

Battesimo refers to the Christian rite of baptism and holds deep religious and cultural significance in Italian life. Traditionally celebrated within the Catholic Church, it marks a child's formal entry into the faith and the wider community. In Italy, where Catholicism has shaped social life for centuries, ***battesimo*** is often one of the first major events in a child's life and a powerful symbol of continuity between generations. It is usually celebrated within the first year after birth, often on a Sunday. Godparents, known as the *padrino* and *madrina*, are chosen by the child's parents. Their role is not only ceremonial but symbolic, representing moral guidance and lifelong support. After the church ceremony, families gather for a celebratory meal, either at home or in a restaurant. These gatherings can be elaborate, with multiple courses, wine, and a decorated cake. As a guest, you will likely receive *bomboniere*, which are small party favors containing sugared almonds, *confetti* in Italian. *Bomboniere* symbolize health, happiness, and prosperity. Even in families that are less religious, ***battesimo*** is frequently observed as a cultural tradition rather than a strictly spiritual one. ***Battesimo*** reflects core Italian values: the importance of family, shared milestones, and collective celebration.

Caffè sospeso NOUN PHRASE

(kahf-FEH soh-SPEH-zoh)

Pay-it-forward coffee

Caffè sospeso is a tradition born in Naples that embodies generosity, solidarity, and the belief that kindness should be accessible to everyone. This phrase literally means "suspended coffee" and refers to the practice of paying for an extra espresso at a café so that someone who can't afford one may enjoy it later. This custom emerged in working-class neighborhoods, where cafés served as social hubs and coffee was an essential daily ritual. In Italy, espresso is quick, inexpensive, and deeply social. With ***caffè sospeso***, the recipient can walk into a café and ask if a suspended coffee is available, receiving the same experience as any other customer. The gesture of paying for ***caffè sospeso*** is anonymous. This anonymity reinforces trust within the community. During times of economic hardship, the tradition has gained renewed importance, becoming a quiet form of mutual support. In recent years, ***caffè sospeso*** has spread beyond Naples and Italy, inspiring similar initiatives around the world, from suspended meals to books and bus tickets. Despite this expansion, its meaning remains rooted in traditional Italian values: warmth, empathy, and generosity. ***Caffè sospeso*** shows that compassion does not require grand gestures. Sometimes, the smallest acts, like a small cup of espresso, can create trust and connection.

Campanilismo NOUN

(kahm-pah-nee-LEE-zmoh)

Local pride; Attachment to one's hometown

Campanilismo describes a strong emotional attachment to one's hometown, village, or local region. The word comes from *campanile*, meaning "bell tower," which traditionally stood at the center of Italian towns. The bell regulated daily life, signaling work hours, celebrations, religious services, and emergencies. For centuries, daily life revolved around the *campanile* and the sound of its bells, making it a powerful symbol of belonging. ***Campanilismo*** explains why Italians often identify first with their city or region rather than with the nation as a whole. Loyalty to local dialects, foods, festivals, and traditions runs deep, shaped by Italy's long history as a collection of independent city-states. Friendly rivalries between neighboring towns are common and can involve debates over recipes, historical claims, or football teams. While these rivalries can be intense, they are usually rooted in pride rather than hostility. This strong local identity contributes to Italy's regional diversity, where customs and traditions change dramatically from one town to the next. ***Campanilismo*** encourages the preservation of traditions and local knowledge that might otherwise disappear. At its heart, it reflects the idea that identity begins close to home. ***Campanilismo*** reminds people that where you come from matters, and that pride in one's roots is something to be celebrated.

Carnevale NOUN

(kahr-neh-VAH-leh)

Carnival

Carnevale is one of Italy's most colorful and symbolic celebrations, marking the period before Lent in the Catholic calendar. The name comes from the Latin *carnem levare*, meaning "to remove meat," and refers to the abstinence and restraint that take place during Lent. ***Carnevale*** represents a final moment of indulgence before a season of reflection. While celebrated throughout the country, each region expresses ***Carnevale*** in its own way. The most famous ***Carnevale*** takes place in Venice, where elaborate masks and costumes transform the city into a living stage. Historically, masks allowed people to hide their identities and temporarily cross social boundaries, mixing nobility and commoners. ***Carnevale*** is marked by parades, decorated floats, music, and performances that often poke fun at political figures and social norms. Food plays a central role, with sweets prepared only during this season. Treats like *chiacchiere* (fried pastry strips dusted with powdered sugar), *castagnole* (small, round fried dough balls flavored with lemon zest and dusted with sugar or filled with cream), and *frittelle* (soft fried fritters) are typical of this Italian tradition.

> ***Carnevale* for Kids** During ***Carnevale***, Italian children dress up as superheroes, princesses, or animals, or wear classic masks like *Arlecchino* and *Pulcinella*, wearing their costumes to school for the day's celebration.

Colomba NOUN

(koh-LOHM-bah)

Traditional Easter cake

Colomba is a traditional Italian Easter cake shaped like a dove, a powerful symbol of peace and renewal. The word ***colomba*** means "dove" and the dessert is associated with Easter celebrations across Italy. Similar in texture to *panettone*, a typical Christmas cake, ***colomba*** is made from a soft, leavened dough enriched with butter, eggs, and sugar, and typically flavored with candied orange peel. Its surface is topped with almonds and pearl sugar, creating a balance between softness and crunch. While *panettone* defines Christmas, ***colomba*** belongs to Easter and the arrival of spring. The cake became widely popular in the twentieth century. ***Colomba*** is rarely eaten casually; it appears at the end of Easter lunch, sliced and shared among family and guests, often accompanied by coffee, sweet wine, or liqueur. Its presence signals celebration and togetherness, reinforcing the importance of shared meals in Italy. Like many Italian holiday foods, ***colomba*** carries a strong meaning. It is tied to childhood memories, family gatherings, and seasonal rituals that repeat year after year. In modern Italy, artisanal bakeries produce elaborate versions of ***colomba*** with pistachio, chocolate, or cream fillings, while still respecting the traditional dove shape and symbolism. ***Colomba*** reflects the Italian way of celebrating through food that carries history, faith, and emotion. It is a reminder that holidays are meant to be celebrated with those you love.

Colpo d'aria NOUN PHRASE

(KOHL-poh DAH-ree-ah)

Draft of air; Sudden chill

Colpo d'aria literally means "blow of air" and refers to the belief that sudden exposure to cold air can cause illness. In Italian culture, this idea is taken seriously, especially among older generations, and continues to influence everyday habits. An open window, air conditioning, or a breeze on the neck is often blamed for headaches, stiff muscles, sore throats, or colds. While modern medicine may challenge the idea, ***colpo d'aria*** remains deeply rooted in daily life. Parents remind children to cover their shoulders, scarves are worn in mild weather, and windows are quickly closed if someone is sweating. These behaviors reflect an emphasis on prevention rather than cure, a value common in Italian approaches to health. Avoiding extreme cold temperatures, protecting the body, and respecting its sensitivity are seen as acts of care. ***Colpo d'aria*** is often mentioned casually in conversation, but it reveals how cultural beliefs shape behavior more than scientific explanations. Even Italians who laugh about the concept may still instinctively act to avoid it, showing how tradition and habit persist. This phrase also reflects a broader attentiveness to physical well-being and balance. ***Colpo d'aria*** is less about medical accuracy and more about inherited wisdom, concern, and protection. It highlights how language preserves cultural attitudes toward health, comfort, and the body, passing them from one generation to the next.

Confetti NOUN

(kohn-FEHT-tee)

Sugar-coated almonds

In Italy, ***confetti*** are not paper decorations, but sugar-coated almonds given to celebrate important life events. They are traditionally offered at weddings, baptisms, confirmations, graduations, and anniversaries. Each almond represents the bittersweet nature of life, while the sugar coating symbolizes the hope that sweetness will prevail. ***Confetti*** are usually presented in odd numbers, most commonly five, representing health, wealth, happiness, fertility, and longevity. ***Confetti*** are usually wrapped in tulle or elegant boxes called *bomboniere* and given to guests as a token of gratitude. The color of ***confetti*** plays a symbolic role: white for weddings, pink or blue for baptisms, red for graduations, and silver or gold for anniversaries. Choosing ***confetti*** is considered an important part of event planning, reflecting the Italian love for detail and symbolism. These sweets are not meant for casual snacking. They are reserved for meaningful occasions and tied closely to shared celebrations. ***Confetti*** transform a simple almond into a symbol of good wishes and joy, turning achievements into moments shared with family and friends.

Not What You Think In Italian, ***confetti*** are sugar-coated almonds given at weddings and celebrations, while *coriandoli* are the small paper pieces thrown in the air. That's why Italians throw *coriandoli* at Carnival but give ***confetti*** at a *matrimonio* ("wedding") or *laurea* ("graduation").

Corona d'alloro NOUN PHRASE

(koh-ROH-nah dahl-LOH-roh)

Laurel wreath

Corona d'alloro refers to the laurel wreath traditionally worn by Italian university graduates. The laurel plant has ancient roots, symbolizing wisdom, victory, and honor in Roman culture. The word *laurea*, meaning "university degree," comes directly from *laurus*, the Latin word for "laurel." This connection links education to classical ideals of achievement and knowledge. On graduation day, students wear the ***corona d'alloro*** during ceremonies, celebrations, and photographs. Graduation in Italy is a major family event, often followed by large gatherings and meals. The ***corona d'alloro*** represents years of study, sacrifice, and perseverance, as well as a transition into adulthood. Unlike quieter graduation traditions elsewhere, Italian graduations are public and communal. The achievement is seen as shared, reflecting family support and collective effort. The laurel wreath serves as a visible symbol of success and continuity, connecting modern students with old traditions. Even today, the ***corona d'alloro*** remains meaningful, blending academic accomplishment with history, symbolism, and celebration.

Ancient Origins In Italian culture, *alloro* ("laurel") comes from ancient Rome, where poets and heroes were crowned with laurel.

Fare una passeggiata PHRASE

(FAH-reh OO-nah pahs-seh-JJAH-tah)

To take a walk

Fare una passeggiata means "to take a walk," but in Italy it represents a cherished daily ritual rather than simple exercise. The *passeggiata* ("walk") usually takes place in the early afternoon or evening, when people stroll through town centers, piazzas, parks, or seaside promenades. It is a social activity meant for conversation and observation. The pace is unhurried, and the goal is presence, not destination. Families, couples, and friends walk together, greeting neighbors and enjoying the atmosphere. If you join a *passeggiata*, you will notice that people dress neatly, even for a casual stroll, reflecting the Italian pride in appearance and respect for public space. Historically, the *passeggiata* ("walk") allowed communities to maintain social ties and reinforced a sense of belonging. It continues today as a moment to slow down in a fast-paced world. ***Fare una passeggiata*** reflects the Italian philosophy of balance between movement and leisure. It values time spent together and appreciation of surroundings. More than a habit, it is a mindset that encourages connection and enjoyment of everyday life.

Flexible *Fare* In Italian, *fare* combines with many nouns to create everyday expressions, often where English uses different verbs: ***fare una passeggiata*** ("to take a walk"), *fare colazione* ("to have breakfast"), *fare una domanda* ("to ask a question"), *fare un errore* ("to make a mistake"), *fare rumore* ("to make noise").

Ferragosto NOUN

(fehr-rah-GOH-stoh)

August holiday

Ferragosto, celebrated on August 15 (*15 agosto*), is one of Italy's most important national holidays and marks the height of summer. Its origins date back to ancient Rome, when Emperor Augustus declared a period of rest after intense agricultural labor. Later, the holiday became associated with the Catholic Feast of the Assumption. Over time, ***Ferragosto*** evolved into a celebration of rest, travel, and togetherness. On ***Ferragosto***, cities often empty as Italians head to the sea, mountains, or countryside. Beaches fill with families, friends gather for barbecues and picnics, and fireworks light up the night. Many businesses close, reinforcing the idea of a collective national pause. ***Ferragosto*** represents a break from routine and a chance to recharge. More than a date, ***Ferragosto*** is a feeling for many Italians: summer at its fullest, marked by freedom and a shared day together. It reflects the Italian belief that rest is essential and that life should include moments of celebration and balance.

From *Agosto* to August *Agosto* comes from *Augusto* (Augustus, the first Roman emperor). This month was renamed in his honor in ancient Rome, just like *luglio* ("July") was named after Julius Caesar, reflecting the Roman roots still present in the Italian calendar.

Festa dei Lavoratori NOUN PHRASE

(FEH-stah day lah-voh-rah-TOH-ree)

Labor Day

Festa dei Lavoratori is celebrated on May 1 and honors workers, labor rights, and the dignity of work. Like International Workers' Day observed worldwide, its origins lie in the late nineteenth-century labor movement, particularly the struggle for fair wages, shorter working hours, and safer conditions. In Italy, the holiday gained strong symbolic importance after World War II, when the country rebuilt itself as a democratic republic grounded in social justice and constitutional rights. Historically, Italian workers, especially farmers and factory laborers, played a crucial role in shaping modern Italy, and ***Festa dei Lavoratori*** serves as a reminder of those collective efforts. Traditionally, the day includes political demonstrations, union-organized marches, and public speeches, especially in large cities like Rome, Milan, and Turin. However, it is also a day of leisure. Many Italians take advantage of the spring weather to enjoy picnics, countryside trips, or time with family. One of the most iconic traditions is the *Concerto del Primo Maggio* ("Concert of May 1"), a free, all-day music concert held in Rome and broadcast nationally. During the event, workers' rights, inequality, and youth issues are usually addressed in speeches and songs. ***Festa dei Lavoratori*** reinforces solidarity across generations and professions, honoring past struggles and present challenges. It reminds Italians that progress is collective and that rights must be remembered to be preserved.

Festa dell'Immacolata Concezione NOUN PHRASE

(FEH-stah dell ee-mahk-koh-LAH-tah kohn-tseh-TSYOH-neh)

Feast of the Immaculate Conception

Celebrated on December 8, the ***Festa dell'Immacolata Concezione*** commemorates the Catholic doctrine that the Virgin Mary was conceived without original sin. In Italy, where Catholicism has shaped history, art, and daily life, this day holds both religious and cultural importance. Religiously, the day is marked by special masses, church services, and processions throughout the country. In Rome, the Pope traditionally pays tribute at the statue of the Virgin Mary in Piazza di Spagna, an event followed closely by many. ***Festa dell'Immacolata Concezione*** emphasizes grace and hope, values deeply embedded in Italian religious culture. Beyond its spiritual meaning, ***Festa dell'Immacolata Concezione*** also marks the unofficial beginning of the Christmas season. On this day, many families decorate their Christmas trees, set up the *presepe* ("Nativity scene"), and begin preparing for the holidays. City centers become festive, shops light up, and Christmas markets begin to appear. This day creates a bridge between reflection and celebration. Traditionally, it is also a day spent with family. You may see many Italians enjoy a long lunch together or take advantage of the public holiday to relax. Culturally, ***Festa dell'Immacolata Concezione*** reflects Italy's ability to merge faith with everyday life. It represents continuity, tradition, and preparation for Christmas and for togetherness. This holiday shows how religious observance, seasonal rhythm, and family customs blend together in Italian culture.

Festa della Repubblica NOUN PHRASE

(FEH-stah DEL-lah reh-POOB-blee-kah)

Republic Day

Festa della Repubblica, celebrated on June 2, commemorates the historic 1946 referendum in which Italians voted to abolish the monarchy and establish a republic. This decision marked a turning point after the devastation of World War II and the fall of Fascism. For the first time, women were allowed to vote nationwide, making the referendum a milestone in democratic participation. This important day is marked by formal ceremonies, most notably a grand military parade along *Via dei Fori Imperiali* ("Street of the Imperial Forums," the grand boulevard linking the Colosseum to Piazza Venezia) in Rome, attended by the President of the Republic. A wreath is laid at the Tomb of the Unknown Soldier, honoring those who died for Italy. Across the country, museums, monuments, and government buildings are often open to the public. Concerts, cultural events, and flag displays reinforce national pride. Unlike more emotional holidays, ***Festa della Repubblica*** has a reflective tone. It reminds Italians that their modern nation was born through civic decision. ***Festa della Repubblica*** emphasizes democracy as a living commitment, connecting past sacrifice with present freedoms.

A National Celebration in the Sky During ***Festa della Repubblica***, Italy celebrates with a military parade and a spectacular flyover by the *Frecce Tricolori*, whose jets release green, white, and red smoke over Rome to honor the Italian Republic.

Festa della vendemmia NOUN PHRASE

(FEH-stah DEL-lah vehn-DEHM-mee-ah)

Grape harvest festival

Festa della vendemmia celebrates the grape harvest, a moment that is tied to Italy's agricultural roots and winemaking. Held between late summer and early fall, the festival varies by region, reflecting local traditions and grape varieties. Pronounced rhythmically, *vendemmia* comes from the Latin *vindemia*, meaning "grape harvest." Historically, the *vendemmia* was a period of intense communal labor. Families, neighbors, and seasonal workers gathered to harvest grapes by hand. When the work was finished, celebrations followed, marking gratitude for the harvest and hope for a good wine year. Today, many towns host festivals featuring wine tastings, parades, folk music, traditional costumes, and reenactments of old harvesting methods. As a visitor, you can participate in grape stomping, cellar tours, and traditional dinners. While modern machinery has changed winemaking, the symbolic importance of the *vendemmia* remains strong in Italy. Culturally, the *festa* represents patience, collaboration, and respect for nature's rhythms. Wine is not just a product, but a cultural expression shaped by land, climate, and human care. ***Festa della vendemmia*** celebrates transformation, from grape to wine, labor to reward, tradition to continuity. This tradition reflects Italy's deep bond with the land and the belief that good things take time.

Festa di San Lorenzo NOUN PHRASE

(FEH-stah dee sahn loh-REHN-tsoh)

Festival of Saint Lawrence

Celebrated on August 10, ***Festa di San Lorenzo*** honors Saint Lawrence, a Christian martyr of the third century. The night is famously associated with shooting stars, known in Italian as *le stelle di San Lorenzo.* According to tradition, the meteors seen during this period are called the saint's "tears." During this time, Italians often gather outdoors on beaches, hills, or balconies to watch the sky and make wishes. This practice blends religious belief with folklore and romantic imagination. Many towns celebrate with evening festivals, candlelit streets, open-air dinners, and live music. During the ***Festa di San Lorenzo***, churches hold solemn services commemorating the martyrdom of Saint Lawrence, particularly in basilicas dedicated to him, where special evening masses draw large congregations. After the services, the celebration moves outdoors, blending the sacred with the festive in characteristically Italian fashion. Culturally, *San Lorenzo* represents hope, sacrifice, and the desire to find meaning beyond daily life. It's a moment to pause, look upward for shooting stars, and reflect. ***Festa di San Lorenzo*** shows how Italian traditions often merge faith, nature, and emotion into shared experiences that feel timeless.

DEE not DIE **When you pronounce this phrase, remember that the Italian preposition *di* is pronounced (*DEE*). The *i* is a clear "ee" sound; it's never "die" or "dee-uh."**

Festival di Sanremo NOUN PHRASE

(FEH-stee-vahl dee sahn-REH-moh)

Sanremo Music Festival

The ***Festival di Sanremo*** is Italy's most famous music competition, held annually in the city of Sanremo on the Ligurian coast since 1951. Originally inspired by European song contests, the ***Festival di Sanremo*** quickly became a national cultural institution and the precursor to the Eurovision Song Contest, which was modeled on its format. This festival is not merely a musical contest but a social phenomenon, bringing together artists, TV personalities, journalists, and viewers across generations. Contestants compete with original songs. Over the decades, the ***Festival di Sanremo*** has launched the careers of Italian icons such as Domenico Modugno, Toto Cutugno, and Laura Pausini. Traditionally, the festival takes place over several nights in late February, broadcast live on Rai 1, the national public TV network. Audiences follow performances and vote for the winners. The festival reflects contemporary Italy and generational trends, while also maintaining continuity with the Italian tradition of lyrical composition and poetic storytelling. Culturally, the ***Festival di Sanremo*** embodies more than music. It represents national pride, creativity, and the power of performance to connect with people emotionally. For Italians, following the ***Festival di Sanremo*** is a ritual: It's a shared cultural experience that combines entertainment with identity. Beyond competition, the ***Festival di Sanremo*** remains a celebration of Italian artistry, language, and the capacity of music to unite a nation, season after season.

Festival di Venezia NOUN PHRASE

(FEH-stee-vahl dee veh-NEH-tsee-ah)

Venice Film Festival

Founded in 1932, the ***Festival di Venezia*** is the oldest international film festival in the world, held annually on the Lido island of Venice. This festival was created to celebrate cinematic art, and over the decades it has become a globally recognized stage for premieres, awards, and artistic innovation. The *Leone d'Oro* ("Golden Lion") is the festival's highest honor, awarded to films of exceptional creativity and impact. During this event, Venice attracts filmmakers, actors, producers, critics, and audiences from around the world, blending cinema with glamour. Screenings occur in historic venues, including the *Palazzo del Cinema*, while events in the canals symbolize Venice's blend of tradition and modernity. Traditionally, the festival takes place in late August or early September. Italian directors such as Federico Fellini, Michelangelo Antonioni, and Paolo Sorrentino have been celebrated at Venice, solidifying its reputation as a bridge between Italian and international cinema. Culturally, ***Festival di Venezia*** reflects Italy's artistic heritage, blending architecture, history, and performance, emphasizing the importance of storytelling. For Italians and international visitors alike, it represents the meeting of tradition and innovation, celebrating film as both entertainment and a reflection of society. The festival also enhances Venice's cultural tourism, making it a symbol of Italian creativity on the global stage. Beyond awards and premieres, ***Festival di Venezia*** symbolizes the connection between Italian culture and world art.

Formula 1 NOUN

(FOR-moo-lah OON-oh)

Formula One racing

Formula 1 is the pinnacle of international motorsport, with a particularly special place in Italian culture due to the legendary Ferrari racing team. Italy has been central to ***Formula 1*** since the mid-twentieth century, producing iconic drivers, engineers, and cars that have shaped the sport globally. Notably, Italian engineers have contributed innovations in aerodynamics, engine design, and safety. The Italian Grand Prix at Monza, near Milan, is one of ***Formula 1***'s oldest and most revered circuits, first run in 1922. The city of Monza attracts tens of thousands of fans, known as *tifosi*, whose passion for Ferrari creates an unforgettable atmosphere. Italians decorate stands with red flags and cheer as the roar of engines, precise pit stops, and victories of drivers evoke national pride. Traditionally, ***Formula 1*** races combine technology, strategy, and athletic skills. Ferrari's legacy, from the 1950s to today, embodies Italian craftsmanship, speed, and aesthetic excellence. For Italians, ***Formula 1*** is more than entertainment; it is a ritual of identity, excitement, and admiration.

Giorno di Ognissanti NOUN PHRASE

(JOR-noh dee ohn-yees-SAHN-tee)

All Saints' Day

The ***Giorno di Ognissanti*** is the Italian name for All Saints' Day, also *Giorno di Tutti i Santi*, celebrated on November 1. It is a national holiday in Italy dedicated to honoring all Christian saints, both known and unknown. The day holds strong religious significance and is linked to remembrance and tradition. Historically, ***Giorno di Ognissanti*** was established by the Catholic Church to recognize saints who may not have their own feast days. Over time, it became an important moment in the liturgical calendar, emphasizing holiness and spiritual continuity. In Italy, the holiday is also culturally connected to the remembrance of the dead, which continues on November 2 with the *Commemorazione dei Defunti*. On ***Giorno di Ognissanti***, many Italians attend church services and visit cemeteries, bringing flowers to graves and honoring loved ones. The atmosphere is generally reflective rather than festive. If you visit Italy on this day, you will notice families gathering quietly, and daily routines slowing down in observance of the holiday. The ***Giorno di Ognissanti*** reflects Italy's deep-rooted Catholic heritage and its emphasis on honoring both faith and family history.

A Small but Powerful Word *Ogni* means "every" or "each" and is invariable (it never changes form). It's used before singular nouns: *ogni giorno* ("every day"), *ogni persona* ("every person"). It's pronounced *(ohn-yee)*, as one smooth sound, not *(og-nee)*.

Giro d'Italia NOUN PHRASE

(JEE-roh dee-tah-LEE-ah)

Tour of Italy cycling race

The ***Giro d'Italia*** is Italy's famous cycling race and one of the sport's three Grand Tours, alongside the *Tour de France* and *Vuelta a España*. First held in 1909, the ***Giro d'Italia*** celebrates endurance, strategy, and the landscapes of Italy, from Alpine peaks to coastlines. Historically, the ***Giro d'Italia*** promoted not only sport but also tourism, highlighting Italy's diverse regions. Cyclists compete over three weeks, facing mountain climbs and flat sprints. Towns along the route host crowds, parades, and local celebrations, blending sport with community spirit. Iconic climbs, such as the *Passo dello Stelvio* ("Stelvio Pass"), challenge athletes. This race embodies discipline, teamwork, and patience. Italian cycling legends like Gino Bartali (1936, 1937, and 1946) and Fausto Coppi (1940, 1947, 1949, 1952, and 1953) became national heroes, as their victories in this race symbolize resilience during and after wartime. Today, fans follow live broadcasts, social media updates, and roadside gatherings, maintaining the popularity of ***Giro d'Italia*** across generations. This event links sport to landscape, history, and identity, showing that competition can be a shared national experience. Beyond medals, the *Giro* invites you to discover Italian geography and hospitality one stage at a time.

How Far Is It? The ***Giro d'Italia*** covers roughly 3,000–3,500 kilometers. It's made up of twenty-one stages, including flat stages, mountain climbs, and time trials, crossing much of Italy from north to south.

Intimo rosso a Capodanno NOUN PHRASE

(EEN-tee-moh ROHS-soh ah kah-poh-DAHN-noh)

Red underwear on New Year's Eve

Wearing red underwear on New Year's Eve is a beloved Italian superstition believed to bring luck, love, and prosperity for the coming year. The custom draws on a long tradition of red symbolism in Italian culture, from ancient Rome to the medieval period, where the color represented power, protection, and vitality. During the nineteenth and twentieth centuries, the tradition spread across Italy, and it was incorporated into festive New Year's Eve celebrations. *Intimo rosso* ("red underwear") is worn under one's clothing and sometimes gifted as a sign of affection and good wishes. Traditionally, the practice is accompanied by other New Year's rituals, such as eating lentils for wealth, lighting fireworks, and gathering with family and friends. ***Intimo rosso a Capodanno*** demonstrates the Italian love of symbolism and playful superstition. Italians view this tradition as a way to celebrate transition into the new year. ***Intimo rosso a Capodanno*** illustrates how superstition and culture can coexist, transforming an ordinary garment into a symbol of good fortune and continuity.

Just Toss It **The underwear should be new, worn on *Capodanno*, and traditionally thrown away afterward to seal the good luck.**

La Befana NOUN

(lah beh-FAH-nah)

The Befana; The Epiphany witch

La Befana is a traditional Italian figure celebrated on January 6, the Epiphany, marking the end of the Christmas season. The name derives from the Italian word *Epifania*. According to legend, ***La Befana*** is an old woman who visits children on the eve of Epiphany, delivering sweets and small gifts to those who have been good and coal to those who have been naughty. She is often depicted flying on a broomstick, dressed in shawls and rustic clothing, embodying both mischief and generosity. Historically, ***La Befana*** has roots in pagan and Christian traditions. Before Christianity, winter solstice celebrations included gift-bringing female figures, which were later integrated into Epiphany customs. Over centuries, the story became intertwined with the biblical *Re Magi* (the Three Wise Men), who were said to have invited her to accompany them to visit the Christ child. ***La Befana*** declined, later regretting her absence and choosing to deliver gifts to children each year as a form of punishment. The legend is widely known across Italy, with regional variations in the story and depiction of her character. Traditionally, Italian children leave out small treats on the night of January 5, hoping to receive candy, toys, or fruit like mandarins from ***La Befana***. If you happen to be in Italy on the eve of Epiphany, you may find towns transformed across the country, especially in central and northern regions, where Italians host Epiphany fairs and parades. ***La Befana*** reminds children and adults of history, tradition, and shared cultural imagination.

La dolce vita NOUN PHRASE

(lah DOHL-cheh VEE-tah)

The sweet life

La dolce vita literally translates to "the sweet life" but its meaning reaches far beyond a simple phrase. It captures a deeply rooted Italian philosophy centered on savoring life with intention, pleasure, and balance. Rather than chasing constant productivity, ***la dolce vita*** invites you to enjoy the present moment, finding richness in everyday experiences and human connection. Historically, the phrase became widely known in the mid-twentieth century, when it came to represent elegance and style. Over time, its meaning evolved. While it can still suggest glamour, ***la dolce vita*** is not reserved for luxury alone. At its heart, it celebrates the art of living well, regardless of status or circumstance. In daily Italian life, ***la dolce vita*** appears in small, intentional rituals. It might be lingering over an espresso at the bar instead of rushing out the door, taking an evening *passeggiata* ("walk") through the town center, or gathering around the table for long, unhurried meals. Equally important is the mindset behind ***la dolce vita***. It emphasizes presence over perfection and quality over quantity. There is room for beauty, humor, and spontaneity, even on the days that you find most ordinary. Today, ***la dolce vita*** resonates far beyond Italy. Around the world, it has become a symbol of slowing down in a fast-paced society and reconnecting with what really matters. It reminds everyone that joy does not always come from more, but from deeper appreciation.

Liberazione dal nazifascismo NOUN PHRASE

(lee-beh-rah-TSYOH-neh dahl nah-tsee-FAH-shee-zmoh)

Liberation from Nazism and Fascism

Liberazione dal nazifascismo refers to the liberation of Italy from Nazi occupation and Fascist rule at the end of World War II. It is commemorated annually on April 25, known as *Festa della Liberazione*, one of Italy's most important national holidays. Historically, Italy experienced two decades of Fascist dictatorship under Benito Mussolini before the country was drawn into World War II. After Mussolini was deposed in 1943, Nazi Germany occupied much of northern and central Italy, leading to a period of violent repression. In response, resistance movements formed across the country, composed of civilians, soldiers, and workers, united against Fascism and Nazism. These groups, known collectively as the *Resistenza*, played a crucial role. The ***Liberazione dal nazifascismo*** symbolizes not only military victory but also moral and political rebirth. It represents the foundation of modern democratic Italy and directly influenced the creation of the Italian Constitution, which emphasizes freedom, equality, and the rejection of dictatorship. In Italy, April 25 serves as a reminder of the sacrifices made by those who fought for liberty. This day is marked by ceremonies, speeches, concerts, and marches throughout Italy. The Italian president and public officials lay wreaths at monuments honoring fallen resistance fighters. While the day can still provoke political debate, its core message remains widely recognized: the importance of remembering history in order to protect democratic values.

Mercatini natalizi **NOUN PHRASE**

(mehr-kah-TEE-nee nah-tah-LEE-tsee)

Christmas markets

Mercatini natalizi are traditional Christmas markets held during the Advent season, typically from late November through December. These festive markets transform town squares into lively spaces filled with wooden stalls, lights, music, and seasonal foods. While especially popular in northern Italy, the ***mercatini natalizi*** can be found across the country, each one reflecting local customs and regional identity. The tradition has roots in central Europe, particularly in German-speaking regions. In fact, the most famous ***mercatini natalizi*** are found in the Alpine region of Trentino-Alto Adige, where cities like Bolzano and Trento host markets inspired by Austrian and German models. However, the concept has been adapted to Italian tastes across many regions, and reflects Italy's ability to blend external influences with its own traditions. ***Mercatini natalizi*** typically feature handcrafted goods, including wooden toys, ornaments, candles, textiles, and Nativity figurines. Food plays a central role as well. Visitors can enjoy *caldarroste* ("roasted chestnuts"), sweets, local cheeses, cured meats, and warm drinks such as *vin brulé*, a spiced mulled wine. Beyond commerce, ***mercatini natalizi*** create a sense of community. Families stroll through the stalls, children meet *Babbo Natale* ("Santa Claus"), and musicians perform holiday songs. The markets offer a slower way of experiencing the Christmas season. ***Mercatini natalizi*** are not just shopping destinations but social spaces where traditions, celebrations, and people come together.

Mercato settimanale NOUN PHRASE

(mehr-KAH-toh set-tee-mah-NAH-leh)

Weekly market

The ***mercato settimanale***, or weekly market, is a fundamental feature of Italian daily life and local culture. Held on a specific day each week in towns and neighborhoods across Italy, these open-air markets serve as important social and economic hubs. Streets fill with stalls selling fresh food, clothing, household goods, and regional specialties. Historically, weekly markets have existed since medieval times, when towns were granted the right to host markets as a way to stimulate trade and community interaction. This tradition continues today, maintaining a direct connection between producers and consumers. Farmers, fishmongers, bakers, and artisans sell their goods directly. At a ***mercato settimanale***, food is central. Shoppers browse seasonal fruits and vegetables, cheeses, olives, bread, and cured meats, often sampling products before purchasing. Bargaining is common, especially for nonfood items such as clothing or accessories, and friendly banter between vendors and customers adds to the atmosphere. The weekly market also plays an important social role. It is a place to meet neighbors, exchange news, and maintain community ties. Elderly residents, families, and young people gather, making the market a shared space that transcends generations. Even in modern cities with supermarkets and online shopping, the ***mercato settimanale*** remains deeply valued. More than a place to shop, the weekly market is a living expression of Italian communal life.

Natale con i tuoi, Pasqua con chi vuoi PROVERB

(nah-TAH-leh kohn ee TWAH-ee, PAH-skwah kohn kee VWOY)

Christmas with your family, Easter with whomever you like

Natale con i tuoi, Pasqua con chi vuoi is a well-known Italian proverb that reflects cultural attitudes toward family, tradition, and social freedom. Translated as "Christmas with your family, Easter with whomever you like," the saying highlights the contrasting nature of the two holidays in Italian life. Christmas in Italy is traditionally centered on family unity, home, and continuity. It is expected that people will gather with close relatives and share elaborate meals. *Natale* ("Christmas") carries strong emotional and symbolic weight, often emphasizing obligation and belonging. *Pasqua* ("Easter"), by contrast, is viewed as more flexible and informal. While still an important religious and cultural celebration, *Pasqua* allows greater personal choice. Italians may spend Easter with friends, romantic partners, or on trips, often enjoying outdoor meals or short vacations. The proverb humorously acknowledges this difference, suggesting that Easter offers freedom after the intensity of Christmas family gatherings. The saying also reflects broader Italian social values. It affirms the need for balance between duty and personal enjoyment. ***Natale con i tuoi, Pasqua con chi vuoi*** is frequently used in conversation to justify holiday plans or to comment on social expectations, and it captures a shared cultural understanding of how Italians experience their holidays.

Ninna nanna NOUN

(NEEN-nah NAHN-nah)

Lullaby

Ninna nanna is the Italian word for "lullaby." The expression is embedded in Italian family life and evokes intimacy, care, and emotional security. Often sung by parents or caregivers, a ***ninna nanna*** is usually a child's first experience of music and storytelling. Italian *ninne nanne* (plural form) have a long oral tradition and vary widely from region to region. Some are sweet and reassuring, while others, especially older folk lullabies, contain surprising references to hardship and poverty. These elements reflect historical realities of rural life, where lullabies sometimes served as emotional outlets for adults as much as calming tools for children. Despite this, the melody and tone remain soothing. Linguistically, ***ninna nanna*** is an example of reduplication (or repeated element), a common feature in baby talk across many languages. The repetition of sounds makes the word easy to remember and comforting to hear. In everyday Italian, the term is also used as the verb phrase *fare la* ***ninna nanna***, meaning "to go to sleep" or "to be lulled to sleep." Culturally, the ***ninna nanna*** represents the bedtime routine, and also the bond between parent and child, built through voice and rhythm. For many Italians, a ***ninna nanna*** is tied to memories of home, safety, and early affection. In modern Italy, the concept of the ***ninna nanna*** remains unchanged. It continues to represent care, patience, and emotional presence.

Onomastico NOUN

(oh-noh-MAHS-tee-koh)

Name day

Onomastico refers to the celebration of a person's name day, a tradition rooted in the Catholic calendar of saints. Each day of the year is associated with one or more saints, and individuals named after a saint celebrate their ***onomastico*** on that saint's feast day. The practice reinforces the connection between personal identity and religious tradition. Names are not labels, but rather symbols of protection and spiritual heritage. Celebrations of someone's ***onomastico*** are usually modest. Friends and family may offer greetings, small gifts, flowers, or a phone call. In some regions, especially in the past, the ***onomastico*** was the primary occasion for celebration, particularly when birthdays were not formally recorded. Although the tradition is less prominent among younger generations today, it still remains recognized. Many Italians remember and acknowledge *onomastici* (plural form), especially for common saints such as *San Giuseppe* or *Sant'Antonio*. ***Onomastico*** reflects Italy's blend of religion, tradition, and social connection.

The Name Day of All Name Days The most famous ***onomastico*** in Italy is *San Giuseppe* (March 19), celebrated nationwide and also known as Father's Day. It's especially important for anyone named Giuseppe, Giuseppina, Pino, or other related names.

Palio di Siena NOUN PHRASE

(PAH-lyoh dee see-EH-nah)

Siena's Palio horse race

The ***Palio di Siena*** is one of Italy's most famous and historic events, held twice each year on July 2 and August 16 in the city of Siena, Tuscany. It is a bareback horse race run around Piazza del Campo, featuring riders representing the city's historic districts, known as *contrade*. The ***Palio di Siena*** has medieval origins and is deeply tied to Siena's civic identity. Each *contrada* has its own colors, symbols, church, and traditions, and rivalry between them is intense. Winning the ***Palio di Siena*** brings enormous pride and prestige, often celebrated more than the prize itself. The event is preceded by days of rituals, parades, blessings of the horses, and community gatherings. The race itself lasts only about ninety seconds. Victory or defeat can define a *contrada*'s memory for years. Beyond sport, the *Palio* is a living expression of history, loyalty, and collective identity. It reinforces social bonds within *contrade* and preserves centuries-old customs. The ***Palio di Siena*** demonstrates how tradition, competition, and community intertwine in Italian culture, transforming a simple race into a symbol of belonging and continuity.

Don't Mispronounce This One *Palio* is pronounced *(PAH-lyoh)*. The *gli*-like sound does not apply here: It's two syllables, *PAH-lyoh*, with a smooth *-lyoh* ending.

Pandoro e panettone NOUN PHRASE

(pan-DOH-roh eh pah-net-TOH-neh)

Traditional Italian Christmas cakes

Pandoro e panettone are the two most iconic Italian Christmas desserts, tied to holiday traditions and family gatherings. Both are sweet, yeasted cakes, but they differ in shape and ingredients. Their presence on Italian tables during Christmas is almost universal, and choosing between the two is often a friendly but passionate debate. ***Pandoro*** originates from Verona, in northern Italy. It has a tall, star-shaped form with eight points and a soft, golden-yellow interior. Its name comes from the Italian words *pan d'oro* meaning "golden bread," a reference to its rich color and ingredients, such as butter, eggs, and sugar. ***Pandoro*** does not contain fruit; instead, it is delicate with an airy texture. It's traditionally served dusted with powdered sugar. ***Panettone***, on the other hand, has medieval origins, comes from Milan, and has a domed shape. It's made with candied orange peel, citron, and raisins, giving it a more complex and aromatic flavor. The preparation process for ***panettone*** is long, involving natural yeast and multiple stages of rising, which contribute to its fluffy structure. Because of this complexity, ***panettone*** is often seen as more elaborate, while ***pandoro*** is perceived as simpler and more elegant. In Italian households, ***pandoro e panettone*** are typically eaten after Christmas meals, especially on Christmas Day and during the days that follow. They are accompanied by sweet wines, such as Moscato or *spumante*. In recent years, many variations have appeared, including ***pandoro*** filled with chocolate.

Pasquetta NOUN

(pahs-KWEHT-tah)

Easter Monday

Pasquetta is the informal Italian name for Easter Monday, the day after Easter Sunday. Officially called *Lunedì dell'Angelo*, this day is associated with leisure, outdoor activities, and spending time with friends. While Easter Sunday is usually reserved for formal meals, ***Pasquetta*** represents relaxation and celebration in a lighter, more carefree way. The word ***Pasquetta*** literally means "little Easter" emphasizing its role as an extension of the Easter festivities. On this day, Italians organize picnics, short trips, and excursions into the countryside, mountains, or seaside. A typical ***Pasquetta*** activity is the *scampagnata*, an outing with friends that includes shared food and games. Parks and rural areas are often crowded, weather permitting, as people take advantage of the spring weather. Food remains central to ***Pasquetta***, but in a more informal form. Meals often consist of leftovers from Easter Sunday, such as roasted meats, hard-boiled eggs, cheeses, and traditional cakes like *colomba pasquale*. Grilling outdoors is also popular. The emphasis is on simplicity and sharing rather than elaborate preparation. For many Italians, saying *Che fai a* ***Pasquetta****?* ("What are you doing on Easter Monday?") is a common question weeks in advance, highlighting how important planning this day can be.

Pinocchio **NOUN**

(pee-NOHK-kyoh)

Pinocchio

Pinocchio is one of the most famous characters in Italian literature and a powerful symbol of Italian childhood. Created by Carlo Collodi in the late nineteenth century, ***Pinocchio*** first appeared in 1881 in a children's magazine and was later published as the novel *Le avventure di* ***Pinocchio***. Adapted a few times since then, you may recognize this story, which follows a wooden puppet, carved by the carpenter Geppetto, who dreams of becoming a real boy. At the heart of ***Pinocchio***'s tale is transformation, both physical and moral. Magically brought to life, ***Pinocchio*** begins his journey impulsive, disobedient, and easily influenced. His adventures are marked by lies and poor choices, symbolized by his nose growing longer whenever he lies. This physical consequence has become universally recognized and is often referenced in everyday language to describe dishonesty. Through interactions with various characters, like the *Grillo Parlante* ("Talking Cricket") and the *Fata dai Capelli Turchini* ("Fairy with Turquoise Hair"), ***Pinocchio*** learns responsibility, empathy, and the value of honesty. His ultimate goal to become a real boy is achieved only after he proves his selflessness and care for others, particularly his father Geppetto. In Italian, the phrase *fare il* ***Pinocchio*** is sometimes used humorously to describe someone who lies or behaves childishly. Today, the story of ***Pinocchio*** continues to be read by children and adults, reminding readers about growth, honesty, and responsibility.

Pisolino NOUN

(pee-zoh-LEE-noh)

Short daytime sleep

Pisolino is the Italian word for a "short nap," typically taken during the day. The term comes from *pisolare*, meaning "to doze," and suggests a light, refreshing rest rather than a long period of sleep. A ***pisolino*** usually lasts between fifteen and thirty minutes and is meant to restore energy without causing grogginess. Traditionally, the ***pisolino*** is associated with the early afternoon, often after lunch. In many parts of Italy, especially in the past, daily schedules were shaped around the *pausa pranzo* ("lunch break"), a longer midday break that allowed time for rest. While modern work routines have reduced this practice in large cities, the idea of the ***pisolino*** remains culturally ingrained, especially among children, older adults, and during weekends or holidays. The ***pisolino*** is connected to the concept of well-being. Italians often view it as a healthy habit that improves one's mood. Saying *Mi faccio un* ***pisolino*** ("I'm going to take a nap") implies self-care; unlike sleeping in late, which can be seen negatively, a brief nap is socially acceptable. Children's daily routines often include a ***pisolino***, especially in preschool years. For adults, it may take place on the couch, in an armchair, or even on the beach during summer. In linguistic terms, ***pisolino*** is used in the diminutive form, which adds a sense of affection and lightness.

Ponte NOUN

(PON-teh)

Long weekend created by a public holiday

In Italian, the word ***ponte*** literally means "bridge," but in everyday usage it has a special cultural meaning related to time off work or school. A ***ponte*** refers to a long weekend created when a public holiday falls close to a weekend and people take one or more days off to "bridge" the gap. This practice is extremely common in Italy and plays an important role in how Italians organize their time. For example, if a holiday falls on a Tuesday, many people will take Monday off, creating a four-day break. In this case, Italians say *fare il* ***ponte***, meaning "to make the bridge." Similarly, if a holiday is on a Thursday, Friday may be taken off to connect the holiday to the weekend. ***Ponte*** is especially associated with travel. Italians often plan short trips to visit cities, the countryside, or the seaside. Popular ***ponte*** periods include late April and early May, when holidays such as *La Festa dei Lavoratori* create opportunities for long weekends. The idea of the ***ponte*** also reveals something about Italian attitudes toward work-life balance. While work is important, taking time to recharge and enjoy life is seen as equally valuable. If you are in Italy around a public holiday, you will quickly notice that the conversation turns to one question: *C'è il* ***ponte****, partiamo?* ("There's a long weekend, shall we leave?"). In schools, ***ponte*** is especially significant. Families often organize vacations around school *ponti* (plural form). Although not officially recognized by law, the ***ponte*** is socially accepted and widely practiced.

Presepe NOUN

(preh-SEH-peh)

Nativity scene

The ***presepe*** is one of the most cherished symbols of Christmas in Italy. It refers to the Nativity scene depicting the birth of Jesus, traditionally including figures such as Mary, Joseph, the baby Jesus, the shepherds, angels, and the Three Wise Men. The tradition of the ***presepe*** dates back to the thirteenth century and is attributed to Saint Francis of Assisi, who created the first living Nativity scene in 1223. Unlike the Christmas tree, which arrived in Italy relatively late, the ***presepe*** has historical and religious roots. It is typically set up in homes, churches, and public spaces during the Advent season and remains on display until Epiphany, on January 6. In many households, placing the baby Jesus in the manger is a symbolic act performed on Christmas Eve or Christmas Day. Italian *presepi* (plural form) can range from simple to elaborate. Some families pass down figurines through generations, while others add new elements each year. The ***presepe*** is not only a religious object but also a cultural expression. Building the ***presepe*** together is often an activity that brings relatives together during the holiday season. Children, in particular, play an active role, learning the story of Christmas through hands-on participation. The expression *fare il* ***presepe*** ("to set up the Nativity scene") reflects an Italian way of celebrating Christmas that emphasizes storytelling, symbolism, and community. It is a visual narrative that connects faith and history in a unique Italian form.

Qualcosa di blu NOUN PHRASE

(kwal-KOH-zah dee bloo)

Something blue

Qualcosa di blu is an Italian expression connected to a traditional wedding custom that originates from an old rhyme about what a bride should wear for good luck. You may be familiar with the full tradition, which includes something old, something new, something borrowed, and something blue, with each element symbolizing a positive wish for the marriage. In Italian culture, ***qualcosa di blu*** specifically represents fidelity and purity. The color blue is associated with loyalty and trust, qualities considered essential for a lasting relationship. Historically, blue was also linked to the Virgin Mary in Christian iconography, reinforcing ideas of purity and protection. For this reason, including something blue in a bride's outfit became a symbolic gesture meant to bring stability to married life. In modern Italian weddings, ***qualcosa di blu*** is often incorporated in subtle and personal ways. It might be a blue ribbon sewn into the wedding dress, a piece of jewelry with a blue stone, or blue embroidery hidden inside the gown. Because it is usually discreet, it creates an intimate connection between the bride and the tradition, known only to her and a few close people. The expression ***qualcosa di blu*** also reflects the respect for rituals that blend superstition and symbolism. It shows how even a small detail can carry layers of meaning, transforming an object or color into a symbol of hope and love.

Sagra NOUN

(SAH-grah)

Local food festival

A ***sagra*** is a traditional Italian local festival, usually centered around food, agricultural products, and regional specialties. The word comes from the Latin *sacrum*, meaning "sacred," because early *sagre* (plural form) were connected to religious celebrations and patron saints. Over time, they evolved into community events that celebrate local identity, seasonal produce, and shared traditions. Today, a ***sagra*** typically takes place in small towns and lasts from one to several days. Each ***sagra*** highlights a specific product, such as mushrooms, truffles, chestnuts, olives, pasta, or wine. Signs announcing the event often read ***Sagra*** *del* . . . ("Festival of . . .") followed by the featured element. Visitors can taste traditional dishes prepared according to local recipes, often made by volunteers from the community. Food is the heart of the ***sagra***, but it is not the only attraction. These festivals usually include live music, folk dancing, games, and sometimes religious processions. Long communal tables encourage people to sit together. *Sagre* play an important role in preserving regional cuisine and culinary knowledge. Recipes are often passed down through generations, and the ***sagra*** becomes a way to protect and promote local heritage. For many Italians, attending a ***sagra*** is not just about eating well, but about reconnecting with traditions. Unlike large commercial food fairs, *sagre* are appreciated for their simplicity. Even tourists seek them out to experience the "real" Italy.

Santa Lucia NOUN

(SAN-tah loo-CHEE-ah)

Saint Lucy

Santa Lucia is a beloved figure in Italian culture, particularly in certain regions of northern Italy, where she plays a role similar to *Babbo Natale* ("Santa Claus"). According to tradition, ***Santa Lucia*** brings gifts to children the night of December 12. In cities such as Verona, Brescia, Bergamo, and parts of Veneto and Lombardy, children prepare for her arrival by writing letters, leaving food for her and her donkey, and going to bed early. It is said that children must be asleep when ***Santa Lucia*** arrives; otherwise, she will throw ashes into their eyes to make them sleep. ***Santa Lucia*** is usually depicted as a young woman dressed in white, often wearing a crown of candles or holding a lamp, symbolizing light and vision. In religious tradition, she is the patron saint of eyesight and the blind. In Italy, her figure blends Christian devotion with popular folklore. The morning of December 13 is a moment of excitement for children, who wake up to find gifts, sweets, and traditional treats. Typical foods associated with ***Santa Lucia*** include candies, mandarins, and in some areas, special cakes. Culturally, ***Santa Lucia*** highlights regional diversity within Italy. While she is central in the north, she is less prominent in southern regions, where other figures dominate December traditions.

Scampagnata NOUN

(skam-pan-YAH-tah)

Casual day trip

Scampagnata is an Italian word that describes a casual outing, usually to the countryside, mountains, or a natural setting. The term comes from *campagna*, meaning "countryside." A ***scampagnata*** is typically informal, unstructured, and shared with friends and family. Traditionally, *scampagnate* (plural form) take place during spring or early summer, when the weather is pleasant. They are especially common on holidays like *Pasquetta* or during long weekends, known as *ponti*. People pack food, blankets, and sometimes games, spending the day outdoors eating, talking, and resting. Unlike a formal trip or vacation, a ***scampagnata*** requires little planning and emphasizes enjoyment over organization. Food plays a central role in any ***scampagnata***. Meals are often simple, such as sandwiches, grilled meats, pasta salads, and homemade desserts. If you join one, you will see that ***scampagnata*** reflects an Italian appreciation for nature and social bonds. It values presence over productivity and time spent together over formal activities. In a fast-paced world, the idea of the ***scampagnata*** continues to represent balance and well-being, reminding people of the importance of slowing down and enjoying shared moments with family and friends.

Italian Leisure Words Similar to ***scampagnata***, Italians also say *gita fuori porta* ("short trip outside the city"), *picnic*, and *giornata all'aria aperta* ("day outdoors"), all suggesting relaxed, informal getaways.

Scoppio del Carro NOUN PHRASE

(SKOP-pyoh del KAR-roh)

Explosion of the Cart

The ***Scoppio del Carro*** is one of the oldest and most spectacular Easter traditions in Italy, celebrated every year in Florence on Easter Sunday. The expression literally means "explosion of the cart" and refers to a ceremonial event involving fireworks and religious symbolism. At the center of the celebration is a large, ornate cart called the *carro*, decorated with flowers and symbols. Early on Easter morning, the cart is pulled by white oxen through the streets of Florence to Piazza del Duomo, where it is positioned between the Cathedral of Santa Maria del Fiore and the Baptistery. The ceremony is attended by large crowds. During the Easter Mass, a mechanical dove known as the *colombina* is lit from the sacred fire and sent along a wire from the altar inside the cathedral toward the cart outside. If everything goes according to plan, the *colombina* ignites the fireworks on the cart, causing a dramatic explosion of lights, sounds, and smoke. This moment is the symbolic *scoppio* ("explosion"). Traditionally, the success of the ***Scoppio del Carro*** is believed to predict a good harvest and prosperity for the coming year. If the fireworks function properly, it is considered a positive omen; any malfunction is seen as unlucky. For this reason, the ritual is followed with suspense. The ***Scoppio del Carro*** is not just a spectacle, it's also a powerful expression of Florentine identity. This tradition remains a vivid reminder of how Italian cities keep history alive through ritual, transforming old beliefs and traditions into shared modern experiences.

Settimana bianca NOUN PHRASE

(set-tee-MAH-nah BYAN-kah)

Winter week in the mountains

Settimana bianca literally means "white week" and refers to a weeklong winter holiday spent in the mountains, particularly between December and March. Traditionally, the ***settimana bianca*** includes skiing, snowboarding, *ciaspolata* ("snowshoeing"), and other winter sports, but it also involves relaxation, social life, and mountain culture. Popular destinations include the Dolomites, Courmayeur, Cortina d'Ampezzo, and resorts in Trentino-Alto Adige. Families, groups of friends, and school trips often organize their annual ***settimana bianca*** as a highlight of the winter. The expression ***settimana bianca*** can also be used more loosely to describe any winter mountain stay, even if it lasts less than a full week. While skiing is central, food also plays an important role, with hearty mountain dishes enjoyed after a day on the slopes. Ultimately, the ***settimana bianca*** represents a balance between sport, pleasure, and tradition. It is a moment where you can disconnect from daily life, reconnect with nature, and experience winter in a shared way, making it an essential part of modern Italian leisure culture.

Less Work, More Holidays In Italian, *giorni feriali* are working weekdays (Monday to Friday), while *giorni festivi* are holidays or nonworking days, including Sundays and public holidays.

Settimana Santa NOUN PHRASE

(set-tee-MAH-nah SAN-tah)

Holy Week

Settimana Santa, or Holy Week, is one of the most important religious periods in Italy and in the Christian calendar. It takes place in the week leading up to Easter and commemorates the final days of Jesus Christ's life, including his Passion, death, and resurrection. In Italy, ***Settimana Santa*** is marked by a combination of public rituals and long-standing local traditions. The week begins with Palm Sunday, known as *Domenica delle Palme*, which celebrates Jesus' entry into Jerusalem. On this day, Italians bring olive branches or palm leaves to church to be blessed, a custom that symbolizes peace and renewal. The days that follow are characterized by churches offering special services and moments of reflection. The most intense moments of ***Settimana Santa*** occur between Giovedì Santo ("Maundy Thursday"), Venerdì Santo ("Good Friday"), and Sabato Santo ("Holy Saturday"). Good Friday, in particular, is observed with processions, reenactments of the Passion, and marches through historic city centers. In southern Italy, these processions are often dramatic, involving hooded confraternities, statues, and traditional chants. ***Settimana Santa*** is a religious and cultural experience. Even those who are not deeply religious often participate by attending processions or respecting the solemn mood of the days leading up to Easter. Traditional foods also play a role, with meat often avoided on Good Friday and replaced by fish-based dishes. In Italy, ***Settimana Santa*** reflects the connection between faith, history, and community.

Tavolata NOUN

(tah-voh-LAH-tah)

Long prepared table

Tavolata is an Italian noun that describes a long table prepared for a shared meal, involving many people sitting together. More than a physical object, the ***tavolata*** represents conviviality and the importance of eating together. The word comes from *tavola*, meaning "table." A ***tavolata*** is common during celebrations such as holidays, weddings, birthdays, or family gatherings. It may consist of multiple tables placed end to end, creating a single long surface where everyone shares food and conversation. In rural settings, *tavolate* (plural form) are often set up outdoors, especially in warm weather, reinforcing the connection between food, nature, and community. Food served at a ***tavolata*** is meant to be shared. Large serving dishes are placed at the center, encouraging guests to help themselves and interact. This format breaks down formal boundaries and creates a relaxed atmosphere. The focus is not on etiquette but on participation and warmth. The concept of the ***tavolata*** reflects a core Italian value: food as a social bond. The length of the meal is part of the experience, often lasting several hours. Metaphorically, ***tavolata*** can also represent inclusion. If you are *invitato alla* ***tavolata***, it means you are being welcomed into a group. This idea reinforces the symbolic power of the table as a place of equality and connection. In a world of fast meals, the ***tavolata*** stands as a reminder of the joy found in slowing down and eating together.

Tifoso NOUN

(tee-FOH-zoh)

Sports fan

Tifoso is the Italian word for a sports fan or supporter, most commonly associated with *calcio* ("soccer"). The term comes from *tifo* ("cheer"), which originally referred to a state of excitement or fever, and it captures the emotional intensity with which Italians follow their teams. Being a ***tifoso*** is not a casual identity, it is a lifelong commitment. In Italy, *tifosi* (plural) are deeply attached to their local team. Allegiance is passed down from parents to children. Saying *Sono **tifoso** della Roma* ("I am a fan of the Roma team") or *È tifosa del Milan* ("She is a fan of the Milan team") is not just a statement of preference, it's a declaration of identity. In stadiums, supporters sing chants, wave flags, wear team colors, and participate in organized cheering known as *tifo organizzato* ("organized cheer"). The most passionate fans often belong to *ultras* groups, which occupy specific sections of the stadium and coordinate chants and visual displays. Friendly rivalries between *tifosi* of different teams are a constant feature of Italian life, especially in cities with historic clubs. Ultimately, being a ***tifoso*** means participating in a community and it reflects an Italian way of expressing loyalty openly.

More Than a Sport In Italy, *calcio* is more than just soccer; it's culture, identity, and passion. *Tifosi* and their teams live the game intensely, especially in Serie A, the professional league, where soccer shapes daily conversations.

Tombola NOUN

(TOM-boh-lah)

Italian bingo game

Tombola is a traditional Italian game similar to bingo, played especially during the Christmas season. It is enjoyed with family and friends during holiday gatherings, and it uses numbered cards and small tokens. ***Tombola*** is played with numbers from 1 to 90, which are drawn randomly and announced aloud. Players mark the numbers on their cards, aiming to complete specific combinations. These include *ambo* ("two numbers"), *terno* ("three"), *quaterna* ("four"), *cinquina* ("five"), and finally ***tombola***, when all numbers on a card are marked. Each stage may be associated with small prizes. One of the most distinctive aspects of ***tombola*** is its connection to the Neapolitan tradition of the *smorfia*, a system that assigns symbolic meanings to numbers. For example, certain numbers may represent dreams, characters, or everyday objects. ***Tombola*** is especially popular on Christmas Eve and Christmas Day, after long meals. It is suitable for all ages, making it a multigenerational activity that brings grandparents, parents, and children together. Even small prizes, such as chocolates, are enough to keep excitement high. Culturally, ***tombola*** represents the Italian ability to transform simple games into meaningful family rituals. If you take part in a ***tombola***, you will see that it is not so much about winning, but about sharing time, laughter, and tradition.

Venerdì 17 NOUN

(*veh-nehr-DEE dee-chee-as-SET-teh*)

Friday the 17th

Venerdì 17 ("Friday the 17th") is considered an unlucky day in Italian superstition, playing a role similar to Friday the 13th in other cultures. The belief combines two elements traditionally associated with bad luck: Friday and the number 17. When they coincide, many Italians consider the day particularly inauspicious. The number 17 has negative connotations in Italian culture dating back to ancient Rome. Written in Roman numerals as XVII, it can be rearranged to form the Latin word *VIXI*, meaning "I have lived" (often paired with "so I died"), a phrase associated with death and tombstones. Over time, this linguistic association contributed to the belief that 17 brings bad luck. Friday, on the other hand, is traditionally linked to negative events in Christian culture, as it is believed to be the day of Christ's crucifixion. The combination of these two elements reinforces the superstition surrounding ***venerdì 17***. On this day, some Italians avoid important decisions, travel, and weddings. The superstition is widespread enough to influence everyday behavior. For example, some hotels skip room number 17. Younger generations often treat it playfully rather than seriously, while others maintain a cautious respect for tradition. ***Venerdì 17*** reflects Italy's relationship with superstition and shows how ancient beliefs continue to shape modern habits.

Vespa NOUN

(VEHS-pah)

Vespa; Wasp

Vespa is an Italian word with two closely related meanings: It literally means "wasp" but it is also famously the name of the iconic Italian scooter you'd see zooming through the country's streets. Produced by Piaggio, the scooter's name comes from its shape and sound, which early observers said resembled a wasp's narrow waist and buzzing noise. Over time, ***Vespa*** has become much more than a vehicle; it is a powerful cultural symbol of Italy, especially associated with freedom, youth, and postwar optimism. After World War II, the ***Vespa*** offered Italians an affordable, practical way to move around cities, and it quickly became part of everyday life. In common usage, Italians often capitalize ***Vespa*** when referring to the scooter brand and use the lowercase ***vespa*** when talking about the insect. The ***Vespa*** scooter is strongly tied to Italian identity abroad. Classic films such as *Roman Holiday* helped turn the ***Vespa*** into an international icon. Even today, riding a ***Vespa*** in cities like Rome or Florence is often associated with a stylish lifestyle.

Iconic Italian Colors These scooters are known for their classic colors, such as *bianco* (white), *nero* (black), *grigio* (gray), *azzurro* (light blue), *verde* (green), and *rosso* (red). These colors contribute to the iconic Italian style.

Idioms and Colloquialisms

Idioms and colloquialisms are the expressions people use instinctively, often without realizing how colorful they are. And they are the heartbeat of everyday Italian. In this chapter, you'll experience the Italian language come alive through phrases that reflect humor, emotion, and cultural understanding. Idioms like *acqua in bocca* or *avere le mani bucate* don't just convey meaning; they paint pictures drawn from daily life. Learning them means going beyond grammar and vocabulary to understand tone, attitude, and intention. These are the phrases you'll hear at the dinner table and in conversations with friends; the sayings that will help you step into the rhythm of spoken Italian.

Acqua in bocca IDIOMATIC EXPRESSION

(AH-kwah een BOHK-kah)

Keep it secret; Don't tell anyone

Acqua in bocca is a vivid Italian expression used to ask someone to keep a secret. Literally, it means "water in mouth," evoking the image of someone holding water in their mouth and therefore being unable to speak. Figuratively, it tells the listener to stay quiet and not reveal any information. This expression is commonly used in contexts among friends, family members, or colleagues. For example, if you are planning a surprise party and want to make sure no one spoils it, you might say, "*È una sorpresa, **acqua in bocca**!*" ("It's a surprise, keep it secret!"). ***Acqua in bocca*** is often used as a stand-alone phrase, functioning almost like a warning. It does not require a verb, and that makes it quick to say. Because of this, it is frequently heard in spoken Italian. While ***acqua in bocca*** is generally lighthearted, it can also carry weight in situations involving trust because by saying it, the speaker is implicitly asking for discretion. Overall, ***acqua in bocca*** is a simple yet effective way to say "don't tell anyone," combining vivid imagery with practicality in a way that feels very Italian.

Allungare il brodo IDIOMATIC EXPRESSION

(ahl-loon-GAH-reh eel BROH-doh)

To drag things out

Allungare il brodo literally means "to stretch the broth," and it's used figuratively to describe making something longer than it should be. In cooking, adding too much water to broth makes it less flavorful. Similarly, in language, ***allungare il brodo*** refers to adding unnecessary details, stretching out a story, and diluting the core message. For example, if someone keeps talking without saying anything important, you might comment, "*Sta solo allungando il brodo*" ("He's just dragging things out"). It can also be used when someone avoids getting to the point, especially in explanations, excuses, or speeches. Grammatically, the verb *allungare* can be conjugated according to the subject and tense. Despite this flexibility, however, the expression maintains its figurative meaning regardless of context. ***Allungare il brodo*** reflects the importance Italians place on substance and authenticity; just as good food should be rich and flavorful, good communication should be direct and meaningful. ***Allungare il brodo*** criticizes anything that feels artificial or unnecessarily extended, making it a sharp and expressive idiom in everyday Italian.

Opposites ***Allungare*** **means to lengthen, stretch, or make something longer, while** ***accorciare*** **means to shorten or make something smaller in length. They're used both literally and figuratively.**

Avere il coltello dalla parte del manico IDIOMATIC EXPRESSION

(ah-VEH-reh eel kol-TEL-loh DAHL-lah PAR-teh del MAH-nee-koh)

To have the upper hand

Avere il coltello dalla parte del manico is a powerful Italian idiom that means "to have the upper hand" or to be in a position of control. Literally, it translates to "to have the knife by the handle," an image that suggests advantage. This expression is used in situations involving power, negotiation, or leverage. For example, in a work context, if one person has important information or authority, you might hear, "*In questa trattativa, ha lui il coltello dalla parte del manico*" ("In this negotiation, he has the upper hand"). The phrase emphasizes imbalance: One party is in control, while the other is at a disadvantage. It can apply to personal relationships, business dealings, and even arguments. Because of its strong imagery, it carries a serious tone. Grammatically, this expression is built around the verb *avere* ("to have"), making it easy to adapt to different tenses and subjects. ***Avere il coltello dalla parte del manico*** reflects a realistic view of power dynamics. Italians often acknowledge when control is uneven, and this expression names that reality clearly. In the Italian language, this common expression is an example of how imagery is used to explain abstract concepts like authority and control.

Avere le mani bucate IDIOMATIC EXPRESSION

(ah-VEH-reh leh MAH-nee boo-KAH-teh)

To be bad with money

Avere le mani bucate literally means "to have holes in hands," and it is used to describe someone who spends money too easily and can't save. The image suggests that money slips through the hands as if they were full of holes. In everyday Italian, this expression is commonly used to comment on spending habits. For example: *Non riesce a risparmiare, ha le mani bucate* ("He can't save money, he's bad with money"). The phrase carries a critical and teasing tone, especially among friends or family. ***Avere le mani bucate*** highlights a lack of financial control and can also be used humorously, acknowledging a personality trait. This idiom uses the verb *avere* ("to have") and a plural noun phrase, *le mani bucate*. It can be used with different subjects and tenses, making it very flexible in conversation. Culturally, the expression ***avere le mani bucate*** reflects everyday concerns about money and responsibility. It shows how Italians talk openly about financial habits, using humor and imagery. This expression turns an abstract concept like overspending into a concrete and meaningful image.

The Short Arm While ***avere le mani bucate*** means to lack financial control, another common expression related to money is *avere il braccino corto*, literally "to have the short arm." It's a playful idiom, meaning to be stingy or very reluctant to spend money.

Avere le mani in pasta IDIOMATIC EXPRESSION

(ah-VEH-reh leh MAH-nee een PAH-stah)

To be closely involved

Avere le mani in pasta is an Italian idiomatic expression used to describe someone who is deeply involved in an activity, situation, or project. Literally, it means "to have hands in dough," an image drawn directly from cooking and baking. In everyday usage the expression often implies that a person is not just involved, but involved in a practical, hands-on way. For example, in a workplace context, you might hear, "*Lui ha le mani in pasta in tutti i progetti importanti*" ("He is involved in all the important projects"). This suggests influence and sometimes authority. ***Avere le mani in pasta*** can also carry a neutral or critical tone depending on context. In some cases, it simply means being busy or engaged in many activities. In others, it can imply meddling or having too much control. For instance, ***avere le mani in pasta*** *dappertutto* ("everywhere") can suggest that someone interferes excessively. This idiom reflects how food imagery is used in Italian to describe work and involvement. Dough is something that must be handled directly to shape the final result, making it a great metaphor for participation and influence. ***Avere le mani in pasta*** captures the idea of being actively engaged rather than passively observing.

Boh INTERJECTION

(boh)

I don't know; Who knows

Boh is a very common Italian interjection used to express uncertainty, doubt, or lack of knowledge. It is the informal equivalent of saying "I don't know" or "who knows" in English. In Italian conversations, **boh** is frequently used on its own as a complete response. For example, if someone asks: *A che ora arriva?* ("What time does he arrive?"), a simple "**Boh**" can mean "I have no idea." It can also be combined with other words, such as **Boh**, *vedremo* ("Who knows, we'll see"). The meaning of **boh** can change subtly depending on intonation. Said flatly, it signals genuine ignorance. Said with a shrug or rising tone, it may suggest indifference. Because of this flexibility, **boh** is very common in spoken Italian but less frequent in formal writing. Grammatically, **boh** does not change and does not require a subject or verb. It functions purely as an interjection, making it quick and expressive. Using **boh** allows speakers to respond without overexplaining.

Buono come il pane IDIOMATIC EXPRESSION

(BWOH-noh KOH-meh eel PAH-neh)

Very kind

Buono come il pane literally means "good as the bread," and it's a very kind compliment in Italian. It describes a person who is genuinely kind, honest, and good-hearted. For example, *Marco è* ***buono come il pane*** means "Marco is very kind." Bread, or *pane*, has deep symbolic meaning in Italian culture. It represents life, simplicity, and community. From the loaves of Puglia to the saltless *pane toscano* of Tuscany, every region has its own variation of bread, but the sentiment remains the same: Bread is a daily staple and a source of comfort. To call someone ***buono come il pane*** is to say they are as genuine and dependable as this most fundamental and nourishing food. The expression can be used for men, women, and even children: *Lucia è buona come il pane* (translating to "Lucia is as kind as can be"). In this case, the adjective *buono* changes to the feminine form *buona* because the subject Lucia is feminine. Ultimately, this Italian idiom reflects an essential aspect of Italian culture: valuing sincerity and simple virtues. It reminds everyone that, like bread, true kindness doesn't need embellishment, it simply nourishes everyone around it.

Capitare a fagiolo IDIOMATIC EXPRESSION

(kah-pee-TAH-reh ah fah-JOH-loh)

To come at just the right time

Capitare a fagiolo is a common Italian idiomatic expression used to describe something that happens at exactly the right moment, often when it is most needed. The verb *capitare* means "to happen" or "to come about," usually by chance, while *a fagiolo* (literally "at bean") adds the idea of suitability. Together, the expression conveys the sense of fortunate timing, when circumstances align in a helpful way. In everyday Italian, ***capitare a fagiolo*** is frequently used to comment on unexpected help, good timing, or an event that improves a situation. For example, if you are struggling to understand a topic and someone offers an explanation, you might say, "*Il tuo aiuto è capitato proprio a fagiolo*" ("Your help came at just the right time"). The expression carries a tone of appreciation, as it implies that things could have gone differently but turned out well. It is typically used in informal spoken Italian, though it can also appear in informal writing. The phrase *capitare proprio a fagiolo* ("to come really at the perfect moment") is very common and adds extra emphasis to this expression. Grammatically, the verb *capitare* can be conjugated in different tenses depending on context, whether you're talking in the past, present, or future. Just as *fagioli* ("beans") added to a dish make it more complete, an event that *capita a fagiolo* makes a moment better and easier.

Casa dolce casa NOUN PHRASE

(KAH-zah DOHL-cheh KAH-zah)

Home sweet home

Casa dolce casa is the Italian equivalent of the English expression "Home sweet home," and it is used to express comfort and appreciation for one's home. In everyday Italian, this expression is often said when returning home after a trip, a long day at work, or an extended absence. For example, after unlocking the door and setting down bags, someone might say with relief, "***Casa dolce casa.***" In this context, the phrase emphasizes the contrast between the outside world and the calmness of home. Unlike many idiomatic expressions, ***Casa dolce casa*** is identical in structure and meaning to its English counterpart, which makes it easy for Italian learners to recognize and remember. The repetition of *casa* reinforces its importance, while *dolce* ("sweet") adds a sense of warmth. This phrase is fixed and does not change grammatically, functioning more like a saying. ***Casa dolce casa*** is widely used in both spoken and written Italian. You may see it on signs or welcome mats, just as "Home sweet home" appears in English-speaking countries. ***Casa dolce casa*** captures how Italians value home as a place of comfort and stability.

A Word with Layers In Italian, *casa* means both "house" and "home." It refers to the physical place and the emotional idea of where you belong: *una casa grande* ("a big house"), *sentirsi a casa* ("to feel at home").

Cento di questi giorni NOUN PHRASE

(CHEN-toh dee KWEH-stee JOR-nee)

May you have many more days like this

Cento di questi giorni is a traditional Italian expression used to convey good wishes during celebrations as birthdays, anniversaries, weddings, or other important milestones. Literally meaning "one hundred of these days," this phrase expresses the hope that the person being celebrated will experience many more days like the current one. The expression is most commonly heard on birthdays. After saying *auguri* ("best wishes"), someone may add, "***Cento di questi giorni!***" In this context, it functions as an optimistic message, focusing not only on the present celebration but also on the future. ***Cento di questi giorni*** can also be used for achievements worth celebrating, such as graduations and anniversaries. In these cases, it highlights continuity rather than a single success. This expression is fixed and usually used as an exclamation. It does not require a verb and it stands alone, though it's frequently paired with *auguri*. The number *cento* ("one hundred") is symbolic, representing abundance and continuity. Culturally, ***cento di questi giorni*** reflects an Italian appreciation for marking time and celebrating life's moments together. It is a simple expression, but one that carries a strong sense of goodwill and shared celebration, making it an essential part of everyday Italian social language.

Che pizza! EXCLAMATION

(keh PEET-tsah)

How boring!

Che pizza! is an informal Italian exclamation used to express boredom, annoyance, or frustration with a situation that feels unpleasant. Despite pizza being one of Italy's most iconic and loved foods, in this expression it takes on a completely figurative meaning unrelated to eating. The phrase is commonly used when facing repetitive tasks, long obligations, or activities that feel boring. For example, someone might say "***Che pizza!***" when talking about a long meeting, excessive homework, or having to wait for something for a long time. In this sense, the expression functions similarly to English phrases like "What a drag" or "How boring." Grammatically, ***Che pizza!*** follows the same exclamatory structure seen in many Italian expressions. It is short, direct, and fixed in form. Because of its casual tone, it is mostly used in spoken Italian and informal writing. If you'd use it in formal or professional contexts it would sound out of place. Understanding how to use this expression prevents confusion, since a literal interpretation of "what pizza" would be misleading.

Say It Like an Italian *Pizza* is pronounced *(PEET-tsah)*. The zz makes a clear "ts" sound, and the vowels stay crisp and clean. It's *PEET-tsah*, not *pee-za* or *piz-ah*.

Che schifo! EXCLAMATION

(keh SKEE-foh)

That's gross!

Che schifo! is a strong and expressive Italian exclamation used to show disgust or strong dislike. Literally translating to "what disgust," the phrase is used to react immediately to something unpleasant. In everyday Italian, ***Che schifo!*** is often heard in reaction to food that has gone bad, something dirty, or an unpleasant environment. For example, opening the fridge and discovering spoiled milk might prompt the reaction, "***Che schifo!***" The phrase is also widely used in a figurative sense. Italians may use ***Che schifo!*** to criticize situations or behaviors they find unacceptable. For instance, hearing about someone behaving badly might elicit the comment, "***Che schifo*** *quello che ha fatto!*" ("How gross what he did!"). In these cases, the phrase expresses moral disapproval. This expression is fixed in form and does not change based on gender or number. The strength of the expression comes from tone and context, and because of its intensity, ***Che schifo!*** is best used in informal settings. It can sound too blunt or inappropriate in formal conversations or professional environments. Among friends or family, however, it is a natural and widely accepted reaction.

The Positive Opposite The opposite of ***Che schifo!*** is *Che buono!* ("How good!") when talking about food, or *Che bello!* ("How nice!") more generally, to simply express approval.

Chi dorme non piglia pesci PROVERB

(kee DOR-meh non PEE-lyah PEH-shee)

You snooze, you lose

Chi dorme non piglia pesci is a traditional Italian proverb that emphasizes the importance of timely action. Literally meaning "Whoever sleeps doesn't catch fish," the saying draws on a simple image: A fisherman who sleeps instead of working will return empty-handed. The proverb is commonly used as advice or mild encouragement. It may be used to motivate someone to wake up early, take advantage of an opportunity, or stop procrastinating. For example, a parent encouraging a child to study or a colleague pushing someone to act quickly might use this expression to underline the consequences of inaction. Grammatically, the proverb uses the impersonal structure *chi* ("whoever") to express a general rule. The verbs are in the present tense, as if the lesson applies universally and always, which is common in Italian proverbs. ***Chi dorme non piglia pesci*** is not meant as an insult, but as a reminder that opportunities require effort and awareness. While Italian culture is often associated with leisure and enjoyment, sayings like this highlight the parallel importance placed on effort and initiative.

Chi la fa, l'aspetti PROVERB

(kee lah fah lah-SPEHT-tee)

What goes around comes around; You reap what you sow

Chi la fa, l'aspetti is a widely used Italian proverb that conveys the idea that your actions have consequences. Literally translating to "Whoever does it, expects it," this expression is applied when someone behaves badly and later faces similar treatment or repercussions. The proverb emphasizes moral responsibility, and in practical usage, ***Chi la fa, l'aspetti*** is often said when an action has a clear cause-and-effect relationship. For example, if someone plays a trick on a friend and then experiences a similar trick in return, another person might comment, "*Vedi?* ***Chi la fa, l'aspetti***" ("See? You reap what you sow"). The expression uses *chi* ("whoever") to generalize the rule, combined with *la fa* ("does it") and *l'aspetti* ("expects it"). ***Chi la fa, l'aspetti*** is typically used in the present tense, reinforcing its timeless quality. While often spoken with an observational tone, it can also carry a warning attitude. For instance, parents might use it with children as guidance, while peers might use it ironically when someone experiences the consequences of their own actions. Culturally, ***Chi la fa, l'aspetti*** reflects a strong Italian awareness of social fairness and reciprocity. Many Italian proverbs emphasize the balance between action and outcome, and this phrase is used across generations, from casual conversation to literature and media, making it a recognizable part of Italian culture.

Chiudere un occhio IDIOMATIC EXPRESSION

(KYOO-deh-reh oon OHK-kyoh)

To overlook something deliberately

Chiudere un occhio is a common Italian idiom used to describe the act of ignoring a fault or minor wrongdoing. Its literal meaning is "to close one eye" and it conveys a sense of deliberate tolerance. It is applied in situations where strict enforcement would be unnecessary, and in everyday contexts, ***chiudere un occhio*** can be used in family, school, workplace, or social settings. For example, a teacher might choose to ***chiudere un occhio*** if a student is slightly late but otherwise attentive. Similarly, a manager may choose to ***chiudere un occhio*** on a small procedural error, recognizing that strict enforcement is not worth the trouble. This expression is made of the infinitive verb *chiudere* ("to close") followed by the noun *un occhio* ("one eye"). The verb can be conjugated to fit tense and subject. For instance: *Ho chiuso un occhio ieri* ("I overlooked something deliberately yesterday") or *Chiuderò un occhio domani* ("I will overlook something deliberately tomorrow"). It is generally neutral, suggesting a pragmatic approach rather than criticism.

Don't Trip on This Sound **The Italian word *occhio* includes a double *c*, which makes a strong and longer *k* sound. It's *OHK-kyoh*, never *oh-chee-oh*.**

Col cavolo IDIOMATIC EXPRESSION

(kol KAH-voh-loh)

No way

Col cavolo is a very common and expressive Italian idiom used to reject a suggestion, request, or idea. It is made of the complex preposition *col* ("with the") and the noun *cavolo* ("cabbage"), so its literal meaning is "with the cabbage," and it relies on food imagery to create a humorous refusal. Despite the literal meaning sounding odd, it is understood in everyday Italian as a strong way to say "Absolutely not" or "Not a chance." In spoken language, ***col cavolo*** is often used in informal situations and it would not be appropriate in a professional setting. If someone asks, "*Vuoi venire a correre domattina?*" ("Do you want to go running tomorrow morning?"), a response of "***Col cavolo!***" conveys strong refusal with a touch of humor. This idiom emphasizes both the speaker's decisiveness and the impossibility of the request. ***Col cavolo*** can be said playfully, with laughter or exaggeration, or more forcefully to express genuine refusal. The listener relies on both tone and context to understand whether the refusal is lighthearted or serious. Culturally, ***col cavolo*** reflects the Italian habit of using food-based expressions metaphorically. Food imagery is often repurposed in Italian idioms to add color and expressiveness to everyday speech. The use of the word *cavolo* here highlights the absurdity of the suggestion being refused, making the rejection memorable and vivid. ***Col cavolo*** is easy to recognize in conversation and can be paired with gestures to enhance meaning, making it both practical and fun to use.

Come i cavoli a merenda IDIOMATIC EXPRESSION

(KOH-meh e KAH-voh-leh ah meh-REN-dah)

Completely out of place; Doesn't fit at all

Come i cavoli a merenda is a vivid Italian idiom used to describe situations, comments, or objects that are completely out of place. Literally, it translates to "like cabbages for a snack" creating a visual image that is absurd: Cabbage is not something you would typically eat as a light afternoon snack. In everyday language, ***come i cavoli a merenda*** is used whenever something seems unrelated to the context. For example, if someone makes a serious remark during a casual joke session, an Italian speaker might comment, "*Quel commento era **come i cavoli a merenda***" ("That comment was completely out of place"). Similarly, an unexpected or awkward action might be described with the same phrase to highlight its incongruity. This idiom is structured as a comparison: *come* ("like") followed by a noun phrase. While ***come i cavoli a merenda*** is generally informal and slightly humorous, it can also be used more critically depending on the speaker's intent. By comparing an incongruous situation to an unusual snack, the expression makes a clear judgment and observation.

Make It Sound Italian The Italian word *come* is pronounced with a hard *k* sound, the *e* at the end is clear, and it's two syllables: *KOH-meh*, never "come" like in English.

Dare buca IDIOMATIC EXPRESSION

(DAH-reh BOO-kah)

To stand someone up; To fail to show up

Dare buca is a widely used Italian idiom that refers to failing to meet someone at an agreed time or place, essentially "standing someone up." The literal translation is "to give hole" but the meaning is figurative. This expression conveys the disappointment or inconvenience caused by someone failing to appear, whether for a date or a meeting. In everyday usage, ***dare buca*** is often applied to social situations, such as romantic dates, outings with friends, or informal appointments. For example, if a friend does not show up for a coffee meeting, another might say, "*Mi ha dato buca*" ("He/she stood me up"). Grammatically, the construction uses the verb *dare* ("to give") plus the noun *buca* ("hole"), forming an idiom. In conversational Italian, it is commonly conjugated to reflect tense and subject: *ho dato buca* ("I stood someone up"), *ti darò buca* ("I will not show up for you"), and so on. It is informal and rarely appears in formal contexts. Culturally, ***dare buca*** reflects Italian attention to social obligations; failing to meet someone is considered impolite, and the idiom captures the action and its social impact in a succinct way. It is widely recognized across regions and age groups.

Same Root, Different Use In Italian, *buco* is a hole or opening in general. For example, *un buco nel muro* ("a hole in the wall"). Meanwhile, *buca* often refers to a pit, dent, or hole in the ground, and it is also used figuratively, as in this idiom.

Dare i numeri IDIOMATIC EXPRESSION

(DAH-reh ee NOO-meh-ree)

To talk nonsense

Dare i numeri is a colorful Italian idiom used to describe someone speaking nonsense and making random statements. Literally, it translates as "to give the numbers," a figurative image suggesting randomness and incoherence. In practical usage, ***dare i numeri*** can refer to verbal or behavioral expressions. For instance, if someone makes illogical claims, one might say, "*Stava dando i numeri*" ("He/she was talking nonsense"). Similarly, it can describe someone acting in a way that is inconsistent or erratic, not just verbally but also in actions. This expression is made of the verb *dare* ("to give") followed by the plural noun *i numeri* ("the numbers"). The verb can be conjugated to match tense and subject: *tu dai i numeri* ("you're talking nonsense"); *loro hanno dato i numeri* ("they talked nonsense"). The idiom is informal and commonly used in everyday spoken Italian. ***Dare i numeri*** can be used lightly to point out someone's confusion or can be used more critically to disapprove of someone's behavior. As with many Italian expressions, this idiom reflects the Italian tendency to use vivid imagery in colloquial speech.

Sound It Out **The Italian verb *dare* is pronounced *(DAH-reh)*. The *a* is open and clear, the *r* is lightly rolled, and the final *e* is unstressed. It's *DAH-reh*, never "deyr" or "dare" like in English.**

Dolce far niente IDIOMATIC EXPRESSION

(DOHL-cheh far nee-EN-teh)

The sweetness of doing nothing

Dolce far niente is a classic Italian expression that celebrates the sweetness of doing nothing. Literally, it translates to "sweet to do nothing" and it's a core aspect of Italian life: valuing moments of relaxation, reflection, and simple enjoyment without guilt (presence over constant productivity). In practical terms, ***dolce far niente*** can describe activities like sitting in a café watching the world go by, lounging in the park, enjoying a slow afternoon with friends, or simply savoring a quiet moment alone. For example, an Italian might say, "*Mi piace il* ***dolce far niente*** *durante il pomeriggio*" ("I enjoy the sweetness doing nothing during the afternoon"). This phrase is not about being lazy; rather it highlights mindfulness and savoring the moment. ***Dolce far niente*** combines the adjective *dolce* ("sweet") with the phrase *far niente* ("to do nothing"), forming a fixed idiom. This expression is informal, often used in conversation and literature. The tone is generally positive and appreciative, and as an expression it praises the balance between effort and rest. This phrase also appears in art, literature, and travel writing as an emblem of the Italian approach to time, pleasure, and social connection.

Essere al verde IDIOMATIC EXPRESSION

(ES-seh-reh al VER-deh)

To be broke

Essere al verde is a common Italian expression used to describe a situation in which someone has no money. The literal translation is "to be at the green." Today, it is idiomatic and understood in everyday conversation. In practical usage, ***essere al verde*** applies to temporary or persistent financial difficulty. For example, after an unexpected expense, someone might say, "*Questo mese sono al verde*" ("This month I'm broke"). The expression conveys the state of having insufficient funds in a colloquial way. Grammatically, the verb *essere* ("to be") needs to be conjugated to match the tense and subject. For example, *noi siamo al verde* ("we're broke"), *io ero al verde* ("I was broke"), or *io sarò al verde* ("I will be broke"). The tone of this expression is informal and conversational. Among friends, it is used with humor to share struggles, while in more serious contexts it conveys genuine economic concern.

Talking About Colors In Italian, *mangiare in bianco* ("to eat in white") means to eat very plain, simple food, like rice, plain pasta, broth, or lightly seasoned dishes, often when you're not feeling well or want something light and easy to digest. For example: *Oggi mangio in bianco perché ho mal di stomaco* ("Today I will eat light because my stomach hurts").

Essere alla frutta IDIOMATIC EXPRESSION

(ES-seh-reh AH-lah FROOT-tah)

To be worn out; To be finished

Essere alla frutta is a widely used Italian expression that describes a state of exhaustion or nearing the end of something. Its literal meaning is "to be at the fruit." This idiom originates from the traditional structure of Italian meals, where fruit is served at the very end. Figuratively, ***essere alla frutta*** suggests that there is nothing left to give, whether in terms of energy, patience, resources, or time. In everyday language, ***essere alla frutta*** can refer to both people and situations. A student after weeks of exams might say, "*Sono alla frutta*" ("I'm completely worn out"). Similarly, the phrase can describe a project, plan, or system that is no longer functioning well, such as: *Questo progetto è alla frutta* ("This project is at its limit"). In both cases, the idiom highlights the idea of reaching a final stage. Grammatically, the expression is built with the verb *essere* ("to be") followed by the prepositional phrase *alla frutta* ("at the fruit"). The verb *essere* needs to be conjugated across tenses and subjects, to match the context, for example: *lei è alla frutta* ("she is worn out") and *loro erano alla frutta* ("they were worn out"). ***Essere alla frutta*** is informal and common in spoken Italian, though it can also appear in journalistic or commentary contexts when describing economic or political situations that are nearing collapse.

Essere come il prezzemolo IDIOMATIC EXPRESSION

(ES-seh-reh KOH-meh eel pret-TSEH-moh-loh)

To be everywhere

Essere come il prezzemolo describes a person who appears everywhere or is constantly involved in many situations. Literally meaning "to be like the parsley," this expression refers to the widespread use of parsley in Italian cooking, where it is added to many dishes. Figuratively, someone who is *come il prezzemolo* seems to be present in every context. In everyday conversation, the expression can have a neutral or critical tone. For example, if a person attends every event, meeting, or gathering, someone might comment, "*È come il prezzemolo, c'è sempre*" ("He/she's like parsley, he/she's always there"). Depending on tone, this can simply observe frequency or criticize excessive presence. This idiom uses the verb *essere* ("to be") followed by a comparative structure with *come* ("like"). It's mostly appropriate in informal situations. Culturally, ***essere come il prezzemolo*** highlights the Italian habit of drawing metaphors from cooking and everyday life (focusing on how often parsley is used in Italian cuisine). Understanding this idiom can help you decode comments about social behavior.

The Opposite of Everywhere ***Stare sulle sue*** **means "to keep to oneself" or "to keep a low profile." It describes someone who avoids attention, doesn't interfere, and stays reserved:** ***Preferisce stare sulle sue e osservare*** **("He/she prefers to keep to himself/herself and observe").**

Essere in alto mare IDIOMATIC EXPRESSION

(ES-seh-reh een AHL-toh MAH-reh)

To be far from being done

Essere in alto mare is a common Italian idiom used to describe a situation that is still far from being completed or resolved. Literally meaning "to be in open sea," this expression draws on nautical imagery to convey uncertainty and lack of progress. Figuratively, it suggests that the goal is still far away and that much work remains to be done. In everyday Italian, ***essere in alto mare*** is frequently used when talking about projects, plans, or preparations that are behind schedule. For example, if someone asks whether a report or assignment is ready, the response might be, "*Sono ancora in alto mare*" ("I'm still nowhere near done"). The expression emphasizes that the work has not reached a concrete or advanced stage. The idiom can be applied to both personal and professional contexts. A student preparing for an exam, a couple planning a wedding, or a team developing a project might all describe themselves as being *in alto mare*. In each case, the phrase communicates delay. ***Essere in alto mare*** is formed with the verb *essere* ("to be") followed by the prepositional phrase *in alto mare* ("in high sea"). In many cases, it is used to manage expectations, signaling that more time or effort is required. Culturally, this idiom reflects Italy's historical connection to the sea and maritime life. The high sea represents uncertainty and distance from safety or completion, making it the perfect metaphor for unfinished tasks.

Essere una capra IDIOMATIC EXPRESSION

(EH-seh-reh OO-nah KAH-prah)

To be ignorant; To be clueless

Essere una capra is an Italian expression that means "to be ignorant," even though the literal translation is "to be a goat." The expression is informal and can sound insulting. Italians commonly use it to describe someone who lacks basic knowledge, particularly in academic or cultural areas. For example, someone might say, "*Sono una capra in matematica*" ("I'm terrible at math"), admitting their own weakness, or "*È una capra in storia*" ("He/she is clueless about history"), referring to someone else. The origin of this idiom is rooted in traditional rural imagery, where goats have been associated with stubbornness and a lack of refinement rather than intelligence. In popular culture, they were seen as animals that eat indiscriminately and act on instinct. Over time, this perception turned the goat into a symbol of ignorance or lack of education. Unlike insults that imply stupidity in general, ***essere una capra*** often suggests ignorance due to lack of study or interest, rather than a lack of intelligence. One important feature of this idiom is how commonly it is used in self-deprecating ways. Italians frequently apply it to themselves to admit a gap in knowledge. When directed at others, however, it can come across as rude and dismissive, especially if said without irony.

Essere una cima IDIOMATIC EXPRESSION

(EH-seh-reh OO-nah CHEE-mah)

To be very smart; To be brilliant

Essere una cima is an Italian idiom meaning "to be very smart," "to be excellent at something," or "to be brilliant." Literally, it translates to "to be a peak" or "to be a summit." The word *cima* refers to the top of a mountain or the highest point of something. Someone who is *una cima* stands above others in skill, intelligence, or competence. Italians use ***essere una cima*** to praise people in many contexts, from school and work to sports and problem-solving. For example, *È una cima in matematica* means "He/she's brilliant at math," while *Sei una cima!* ("You are very smart!") can be used to congratulate someone who has done something particularly well. This expression can also be used ironically, depending on tone. In sarcastic contexts, saying, "*Sei proprio una cima*" ("You are really smart") may imply the opposite, meaning someone has made an obvious mistake. Native Italian speakers rely heavily on context to interpret whether the phrase is genuine praise or not.

Not So Smart *Essere una frana* (literally, "to be a landslide") is a colloquial Italian expression meaning to be really bad at something or a total disaster at it. It's informal and often self-deprecating: *Sono una frana con i numeri* ("I'm terrible with numbers").

Fare il passo più lungo della gamba IDIOMATIC EXPRESSION

(FAH-reh eel PAHS-soh pyoo LOON-goh DEL-lah GAHM-bah)

To bite off more than one can chew

Fare il passo più lungo della gamba is an Italian idiom meaning "to bite off more than one can chew." Literally, it translates to "to take a step longer than the leg"; the vivid physical image makes the meaning clear. If your step is longer than your leg, you will lose balance and fall. This expression is commonly used to warn against overconfidence, lack of planning, or unrealistic ambition. Italians might use it when someone takes on a project that is too demanding or commits to responsibilities they can't manage. For example, *Lui ha aperto tre negozi insieme e ha fatto il passo più lungo della gamba* ("He opened three shops at once and bit off more than he can chew"). While ambition is valued, Italian culture emphasizes balance, moderation, and knowing one's limits. ***Fare il passo più lungo della gamba*** is not necessarily a condemnation of ambition, but rather of imprudence; it suggests that success requires self-awareness and realistic judgment. The expression is informal and used in both spoken and written Italian.

More Meaning *Più* is pronounced *(pyoo)* (one smooth syllable). It means "more" or "plus" and is also used for comparisons and quantities: *più grande* ("bigger"), *più tempo* ("more time"). The final accent shows the stress and keeps it as one syllable, not *pi-u*.

Fare le ore piccole IDIOMATIC EXPRESSION

(FAH-reh leh OH-reh PEEK-koh-leh)

To stay up very late

This expression means "to stay up very late" especially into the early hours of the morning. Literally, it translates as "to do the hours small," referring to the hours after midnight when the numbers on the clock are smaller. ***Fare le ore piccole*** is typically used to describe nights spent socializing, studying, partying, or working late, with the implication of tiredness the following day. For example, *Noi abbiamo fatto le ore piccole parlando* ("We stayed up very late talking"), or *Io ho fatto le ore piccole per finire il progetto* ("I was up until very late to finish the project"). This expression is made of the verb *fare* ("to do, to make"), which needs to be conjugated for tense and subject, and the noun and adjective *le ore piccole* ("the small hours"). This idiom carries a positive tone, usually associated with meaningful or enjoyable experiences, rather than simple exhaustion. Unlike expressions such as *dormire poco* ("to sleep little"), ***fare le ore piccole*** focuses on staying awake rather than sleeping badly.

Before You Say It Out Loud The Italian word *piccole* is pronounced (*PEEK-koh-leh*). The double c makes a strong *k* sound that needs to be pronounced.

Fare una brutta figura PHRASE

(FAH-reh OO-nah BROOT-tah fee-GOO-rah)

To make a bad impression

Fare una brutta figura means "to make a bad impression," but literally, it translates as "to make an ugly figure." In Italy, making a bad impression often implies violating social rules, such as etiquette, manners, or expectations. For example, arriving late to a formal dinner without apologizing, dressing inappropriately for an occasion, or speaking out of turn can all be described as ***fare una brutta figura***. Italians use this expression frequently in both serious and lighthearted contexts. For example, a parent might warn a child, "*Comportati bene, non farmi **fare una brutta figura***" ("Behave yourself, don't make me look bad"). This expression is often contrasted with *fare una bella figura*, its positive counterpart, which means "to make a good impression." While *fare una bella figura* is about elegance and good presentation, ***fare una brutta figura*** represents the fear of public embarrassment. Despite its negative meaning, it is not usually harsh or cruel. Instead, it reflects a shared awareness of social norms and the desire to navigate them gracefully. Ultimately, ***fare una brutta figura*** captures the Italian sensitivity to context, manners, and the role of social perception in everyday life.

Guastafeste NOUN

(gwahs-tah-FEH-steh)

Party pooper

Guastafeste is an Italian noun used to describe someone who ruins the mood or spoils the enjoyment of others. The word is a compound of the verb *guastare* ("to spoil" or "to ruin") and the noun *feste* ("parties" or "celebrations"), making its meaning very transparent: a person who ruins the party. In English, it is often translated as "party pooper" or "spoilsport." This term is used in informal contexts and can be either playful or critical, depending on tone. For example, someone who insists on pointing out problems, rules, or bad news during a happy moment might be labeled a ***guastafeste***. You might hear, "*Non fare il **guastafeste***" ("Don't be a party pooper"), or "*È sempre il **guastafeste** del gruppo*" ("He's always the party pooper of the group"). Calling someone a ***guastafeste*** does not necessarily imply malicious intent. Often, it simply describes someone who is overly serious or pessimistic. Grammatically, ***guastafeste*** is invariable in form: The singular and plural are the same. Context determines number, for example in the plural form, *I **guastafeste** non sono invitati* ("Party poopers are not invited").

Party Pooper versus Life of the Party In Italian, the opposite of ***guastafeste*** is *anima della festa* (literally, "soul of the party"), used for someone who brings energy and keeps things lively. You might hear, "*È l'anima della festa*" ("He/she is the life of the party").

In bocca al lupo IDIOMATIC EXPRESSION

(een BOHK-kah al LOO-poh)

Good luck

In bocca al lupo is one of the most famous Italian expressions used to wish someone good luck. Literally, it means "in mouth of the wolf," which at first glance seems odd. Someone might say, "***In bocca al lupo*** *per l'esame*" ("Good luck on the exam"). The traditional response to ***In bocca al lupo*** is *Crepi il lupo*, meaning "May the wolf die," or simply *Crepi*. Although some people today prefer to answer with "*Grazie*" ("Thank you"), the traditional response remains widely understood and used. The origins of the expression are debated, but it is often linked to hunting and pastoral traditions. One theory suggests that wishing someone to end up "in the mouth of the wolf" meant placing them under the protection of a strong animal. Another interpretation connects it to the idea of facing danger head-on rather than avoiding it. Regardless of its exact origin, the phrase has been part of Italian oral tradition for a long time. ***In bocca al lupo*** is especially common in artistic and sporting contexts, where saying "*Buona fortuna*" ("Good luck") is sometimes considered less appropriate or even unlucky. Actors, musicians, and athletes often prefer ***In bocca al lupo***, seeing it as a sign of shared tradition and solidarity. What might sound negative on the surface, like "Break a leg" in English, actually carries encouragement, protection, and support, making ***In bocca al lupo*** one of the most emotionally resonant ways to wish someone success.

Ma va' INTERJECTION

(mah vah)

Come on; No way

Ma va' is a short but powerful Italian expression used to express disbelief and skepticism. Literally, it means "but go," derived from the verb *andare* ("to go"), yet its meaning is closer to "come on," "no way," or even "get out of here." The phrase is highly dependent on tone and context and can range from surprise to clear irritation. In casual conversation, ***ma va'*** is often used as a reaction to unexpected or unbelievable information. For example, if someone shares surprising news, a listener might respond, "***Ma va'***, *non ci credo!*" ("No way, I don't believe it!"). In this sense, the expression conveys amazement. However, it can also function as a dismissive or annoyed response, especially when paired with certain intonations or gestures. Said sharply, it may imply "nonsense." Because of this flexibility, non-native speakers should be cautious when using it, as the same words can sound friendly or rude depending on delivery. ***Ma va'*** is very informal and is almost exclusively used in spoken Italian. It is common among friends, family members, and peers but generally avoided in formal or professional contexts. Linguistically, its brevity adds to its expressiveness, allowing you to convey an emotional reaction in just two syllables.

Mamma mia! EXCLAMATION

(MAHM-mah MEE-ah)

Oh my goodness!; Wow!

Mamma mia! is one of the most recognizable Italian exclamations worldwide. Literally meaning "my mom," it is used to express a wide range of emotions, including surprise, frustration, admiration, disbelief, or concern. Much like "Oh my goodness!" or "Oh my God!" in English, its meaning depends heavily on tone and context. For example, ***Mamma mia**, che caldo!* translates to "Oh my goodness, it's so hot!" while ***Mamma mia**, che disastro!* means "Oh my God, what a disaster!" Unlike its literal meaning, the expression is not usually connected to one's actual mother. Instead, it functions as an emotional release, allowing speakers to emphasize their reaction to a situation. From a cultural perspective, invoking the mom's image adds emotional intensity without being vulgar or offensive. For this reason, ***Mamma mia!*** is socially acceptable in most contexts and is commonly used across generations. The expression has also been popularized internationally, sometimes becoming a stereotype of Italian speech. While Italians do use it frequently, they tend to do so naturally and sparingly, not constantly as exaggerated portrayals might suggest. Grammatically, ***Mamma mia!*** stands alone as an exclamation and does not change its form depending on who is speaking.

Meglio tardi che mai PROVERB

(MEHL-yoh TAR-dee keh MAI)

Better late than never

Meglio tardi che mai is an Italian proverb meaning "Better late than never," used to express that completing something belatedly is preferable to not doing it at all. The phrase applies to a wide range of situations, from apologies and life decisions to projects and personal goals. For example, someone might say, "*Lui ha finito gli studi a quarant'anni, ma **meglio tardi che mai***" ("He finished his studies at forty years old, but better late than never"). Neutral in tone, this proverb reflects a pragmatic worldview. Rather than focusing on missed opportunities or delays, it emphasizes action and improvement, even if they come late. In Italian culture, ***Meglio tardi che mai*** offers reassurance and encouragement. The expression can also be ironic depending on context. For example, it can be used humorously to comment on small delays, such as arriving late at a meeting. Its flexibility contributes to its frequent use in everyday conversation. Grammatically, this proverb is fixed and does not change. It is widely understood across Italy and across generations, making it one of the most stable elements of spoken Italian. Like many Italian proverbs, it conveys a moral lesson in a concise and memorable way.

Mettere una pulce nell'orecchio IDIOMATIC EXPRESSION

(MEHT-teh-reh OO-nah POOL-cheh nell-oh-REHK-kyoh)

To plant a doubt; To make someone suspicious

Mettere una pulce nell'orecchio is an Italian idiom meaning "to plant a doubt" or "to make someone suspicious." Its literal translation is "to put a flea in the ear," an image that evokes discomfort and irritation. Just as a flea in the ear would be impossible to ignore, the doubt introduced by this expression continues to bother a person, prompting concern. This idiom is commonly used when someone hints at a possibility without offering clear proof. For example, *Loro gli hanno messo una pulce nell'orecchio sul comportamento del socio* means "They planted a doubt in his mind about the partner's behavior." The person who *mette una pulce nell'orecchio* does not openly accuse but suggests that something may be wrong. The expression can be neutral or negative depending on context. It may describe a necessary warning, such as alerting someone to a potential problem, or it may imply manipulation, where doubt is intentionally introduced to cause mistrust. Grammatically, the idiom uses the verb *mettere* ("to put"), which is conjugated based on the tense and subject. It is used in both spoken and written Italian and applies to personal, professional, and social situations.

Mica ADVERB

(MEE-kah)

Not at all; By any means

Mica is a unique Italian adverb used to strengthen negation. While it originally meant "crumb" or "small amount," in modern Italian it functions as an emphatic negative, often translated as "not at all" or "by any means." For example, *Non è **mica** facile* means "It's not easy at all," adding emphasis beyond a simple negative *non* ("not"). Unlike standard negation, ***mica*** is optional and expressive. The use of ***mica*** is primarily informal and conversational. It is common in spoken Italian and informal writing but usually avoided in formal or academic contexts. Interestingly, ***mica*** can sometimes appear without *non*, especially in questions or rhetorical statements, such as "***Mica** vorrai andarci a piedi?*" ("You don't really want to go there on foot, do you?"). From a cultural perspective, ***mica*** reflects the Italian tendency to communicate nuance with small linguistic markers. Because it has no perfect equivalent in English, learners often find it challenging to learn; however, it's commonly used in spoken language and so it is important to understand its use.

Mitico | Mitica ADJECTIVE

(MEE-tee-koh) | (MEE-tee-kah)

Awesome

Mitico is a versatile Italian adjective used to describe someone or something considered exceptional. Literally, it means "mythical," deriving from *mito* ("myth"), but in everyday Italian it often translates to "awesome." The word is commonly used in informal and colloquial contexts as a form of enthusiastic praise. For example, *Sei **mitico**!* can mean "You're awesome!" or "You're a legend!" Originally, ***mitico*** referred strictly to figures from mythology, such as heroes or gods. Over time, its meaning expanded to include real people and situations that leave a strong positive impression. Today, it can describe a person who does a favor, tells a great story, or succeeds in some way. It can also apply to events, moments, or even objects, as in *Una serata **mitica*** ("An amazing evening"). Grammatically, ***mitico*** agrees in gender and number with the noun it modifies, becoming ***mitica*** (feminine singular), *mitici* (masculine plural), or *mitiche* (feminine plural). Overall, ***mitico*** captures enthusiasm and admiration, making it a staple of informal Italian praise.

Pronounce It Like an Italian The Italian word ***mitico*** is pronounced *(MEE-tee-koh)*. The stress falls on the first syllable, *MI-ti-co*, and the "ti" is a clear *t* sound, not "ts" or "sh."

Non avere peli sulla lingua IDIOMATIC EXPRESSION

(non ah-VEH-reh PEH-lee SOOL-lah LEEN-gwah)

To speak one's mind; To be blunt

Non avere peli sulla lingua is an Italian idiom meaning "to speak one's mind" or "to be very blunt." Literally, it translates to "to not have hair on the tongue." The imagery suggests that nothing blocks or softens speech, allowing words to come out directly and without restraint. This expression is commonly used to describe people who are outspoken and honest, sometimes to the point of being tactless. For example, *Lui è una persona che non ha peli sulla lingua* means "He's a blunt person." Depending on context, this trait can be admired as sincerity or criticized as lack of tact. While honesty is valued in Italian culture, if you speak too directly you can create tension. ***Non avere peli sulla lingua*** is often used in discussions about public figures, journalists, or politicians known for direct language. It can also describe personal relationships where openness is prioritized over politeness. This expression is widely accepted and not considered vulgar. Grammatically, it includes the verb *avere* ("to have"), which needs to be conjugated to match the tense and the subject.

Watch Out for These In Italian, *capello* means a single strand of hair on your head (singular; *capelli* is plural), while *pelo* (singular; *peli* is plural) refers to body hair. That's why Italians say *lavarsi i capelli* ("wash the hair") but *togliere i peli* ("remove body hair").

Non c'è trippa per gatti IDIOMATIC EXPRESSION

(non cheh TREEP-pah pehr GAHT-tee)

There's nothing left; There is no chance

Non c'è trippa per gatti is a colorful Italian idiom meaning "There's nothing left." Literally, it translates to "There's no tripe for cats," and it conveys the absence of any possibility, often with a slightly ironic tone. The origin of this idiom is well documented and dates back to the early twentieth century in Rome. Ernesto Nathan, the mayor of Rome at the time, reportedly cut funding for feeding stray cats with *trippa* ("tripe"), a cheap meat product, thinking that they would be more motivated to hunt mice. When reviewing municipal budgets, he is said to have written ***Non c'è trippa per gatti***, meaning there was no money available for that expense. Over time, the phrase entered common usage as a way to express denial or lack of resources. Today, Italians use the expression in both serious and lighthearted contexts. For example, ***Non c'è trippa per gatti*** *se pensi a un aumento* ("There's no chance if you're thinking about a raise"). It implies finality and leaves little room for negotiation. Culturally, the expression reflects Italian creativity in transforming historical anecdotes into everyday language. It also shows how humor is often used to convey firm messages without sounding overly harsh. Overall, ***Non c'è trippa per gatti*** remains a vivid and expressive way to shut down unrealistic expectations or requests.

Non è il mio forte PHRASE

(non eh eel MY-oh FOR-teh)

It's not my strong suit

Non è il mio forte is an understated Italian expression used to admit a lack of ability or confidence in a particular area. It translates as "it's not my strong suit." The expression allows you as the speaker to acknowledge your weaknesses without sounding overly negative. It is commonly used in professional, academic, and social contexts. For example, *La matematica* ***non è il mio forte*** means "Math isn't my strong suit." The phrase often serves as a disclaimer before asking for help or excusing a mistake. Rather than making absolute statements like "I'm bad at this," this expression softens the admission, leaving room for improvement. It can refer to skills, subjects, or even personality traits. Grammatically, the structure is straightforward, allowing different subjects or activities to be inserted easily. The expression ***non è il mio forte*** is an elegant way to communicate limitations while remaining polite, realistic, and socially aware.

What's Your Forte? In Italian, *è il mio forte* means "it's my strength" or "that's what I'm good at"; it's the opposite of ***non è il mio forte***. It's commonly used to talk about skills or abilities: *La grammatica è il mio forte, mentre la pronuncia* ***non è il mio forte*** ("Grammar is my strength, while pronunciation is not my strong suit").

Non tutte le ciambelle escono col buco IDIOMATIC EXPRESSION

(non TOOT-teh leh chahm-BEL-leh ESH-koh-noh kohl BOO-koh)

Things don't always turn out perfectly

Non tutte le ciambelle escono col buco literally means "not all doughnuts come out with the hole," and it is used figuratively to remind people that things don't always go perfectly as planned. The phrase emphasizes that despite preparation or effort, results can vary, and perfection is not guaranteed. For example, in a work context someone might use it to accept a setback gracefully, saying "*Noi abbiamo provato, ma* ***non tutte le ciambelle escono col buco***" ("We tried, but it didn't turn out perfectly"). The expression draws from a literal image: *Ciambelle* ("doughnuts") are supposed to have a round shape with a hole in the middle. In baking, however, sometimes doughnuts come out misshapen or without a perfect hole. This imperfection becomes a metaphor for life's unpredictability. It's a way of accepting failures, or unplanned outcomes, and emphasizing patience and resilience. In modern Italian, you can use this idiom in both serious and lighthearted contexts. Friends might use it jokingly if a plan fails, while adults often use it to convey wisdom about life's uncertainties.

Non vedo l'ora IDIOMATIC EXPRESSION

(non VEH-doh LOH-rah)

I can't wait

Non vedo l'ora literally translates to "I don't see the hour" but figuratively, it expresses excitement for an event, moment, or activity. Italians use it to convey impatience in a positive, enthusiastic way. For instance, you might hear someone say, "***Non vedo l'ora*** *di andare in vacanza*" ("I can't wait to go on vacation"), or a friend might exclaim, "***Non vedo l'ora*** *di vederti!*" ("I can't wait to see you!"). The origin of the phrase comes from the literal idea of not being able to see the hour arrive soon enough: The wait feels long, and the anticipation is intense. It emphasizes emotion and enthusiasm. ***Non vedo l'ora*** is widely used in spoken Italian, and grammatically, the phrase uses the negative form of the verb *vedere* ("to see") with the noun *ora* ("hour" or "time"). Despite the negative *non* ("not"), in context it expresses a positive feeling, an example of how Italian expressions sometimes work contrary to literal translation.

Different Ways to Say It Other ways to express anticipation in Italian include *io sono impaziente* ("I'm impatient") or *io attendo con ansia* ("I'm anxiously waiting"), but ***non vedo l'ora*** is the most common colloquial phrase and conveys both excitement and eagerness in everyday conversation.

Parla come mangi IDIOMATIC EXPRESSION

(PAR-lah KOH-meh MAHN-jee)

Speak clearly; Speak plainly

Parla come mangi literally translates to "speak as you eat," but figuratively it means "speak clearly" or "speak plainly, don't use complicated words." Italians use it to remind someone to communicate in a simple, straightforward way rather than overcomplicating things or using unnecessary language. For example, a person might say, "***Parla come mangi****, così ti capiamo meglio*," meaning "Speak plainly, so we can understand you better." Similarly, among friends, someone might tease, "***Parla come mangi****, non serve fare il professore*," which translates to "Speak plainly, no need to act like a professor." The idiom comes from the idea that eating is an instinctive, basic action; everyone knows how to do it, and it's unpretentious. By saying "***Parla come mangi***," you suggest that speaking should also be instinctive, clear, and understandable. This expression is a playful admonition for anyone trying too hard to impress with complicated vocabulary, technical jargon, or overly formal speech. In everyday Italian, the phrase is lighthearted and usually not offensive. It usually does not appear in professional contexts, but rather in casual settings when someone is over-explaining. It's also used humorously in Italian media, such as movies or TV shows, when a character pretends to be sophisticated but is reminded to keep it simple.

Pieno come un uovo IDIOMATIC EXPRESSION

(PYEH-noh KOH-meh oon WOH-voh)

Completely full

Pieno come un uovo literally means "full like an egg," and it is used figuratively in everyday life to describe physical fullness. For instance, after a large meal, someone might say, "*Sono* ***pieno come un uovo***" ("I'm completely full"). This expression comes from the image of an egg, which is tightly enclosed and full inside its shell. The comparison conveys completeness and sometimes the idea of being overfilled. ***Pieno come un uovo*** carries a lighthearted tone and is generally informal, and it is not used in professional situations. Since this expression uses the Italian adjective *pieno* ("full"), the ending of the word must change when speaking as a female. For example, a woman might say, "*Sono piena come un uovo.*" Other Italian phrases for fullness include *completamente pieno* ("completely full"), but ***pieno come un uovo*** adds idiomatic flavor with a metaphor that is visual and immediately evocative. Another expression that you can use when you're completely full from eating a large meal is *io scoppio*, which means "I'm exploding."

To Explode or Not In Italian, *scoppio* can be a tricky variation of ***pieno come un uovo*** because it works in two related ways: as a noun meaning "explosion" or "burst" (*uno scoppio*), or as part of the verb *scoppiare*, meaning "to explode" or "to burst." Context tells you which meaning is intended.

Saltare dalla padella alla brace IDIOMATIC EXPRESSION

(sal-TAH-reh DAL-lah pah-DEL-lah ALL-lah BRAH-cheh)

To go from bad to worse

Saltare dalla padella alla brace literally means "to jump from the pan into the embers," and figuratively, it describes a situation where someone escapes a problem only to land in an even worse one. The phrase is used to comment on decisions that backfire or worsen circumstances. For example, if someone leaves a stressful job for another that turns out to be even more difficult, an Italian might say, "*Hai cambiato lavoro? Attento a non* ***saltare dalla padella alla brace***" (translating to "You changed jobs? Be careful not to go from bad to worse"). The idiom has its roots in medieval Italy, reflecting the dangers of cooking with open fire and wood embers. Frying pans were often placed over hot coals, and it was easy for food to slip from the pan directly into the embers, trading one kind of heat for something far worse. This vivid image evolved into a metaphor for situations where attempts to escape trouble only create bigger problems. In modern usage, ***saltare dalla padella alla brace*** applies to a wide range of scenarios: personal relationships, work situations, or financial choices. It is a cautionary phrase, which can be delivered with a mix of humor and wisdom. For example, *Hai già bevuto tanto, e sei saltato dalla padella alla brace* ("You already drank a lot, and you went from bad to worse") might be said jokingly to a friend about social decisions.

Stare con le mani in mano IDIOMATIC EXPRESSION

(STAH-reh kon leh MAH-nee in MAH-noh)

To do nothing

Stare con le mani in mano literally translates as "to stay with the hands in hand," and it is used figuratively to describe someone who is inactive, or doing nothing when they should be doing something. For example, if a person is watching a problem developing without helping, an Italian might say, "*Non puoi* ***stare con le mani in mano****, devi fare qualcosa!*" ("You can't just do nothing, you have to do something!"). The idiom comes from the visual image of someone literally keeping their hands folded and doing nothing while action is needed. It emphasizes passivity, laziness, and procrastination. ***Stare con le mani in mano*** is widely used in both personal and professional contexts. A parent might say it to a teenager who isn't helping with chores, while a manager might use it to encourage proactive behavior in the workplace, even though in such a setting it might sound a bit harsh and direct. The phrase also carries a sense of urgency, suggesting that time is being wasted while action could prevent problems or seize opportunities.

A Tricky Feminine Word Most feminine Italian nouns end in *-a*, which usually makes gender predictable; however, *la mano* is an exception, ending in *-o* while remaining feminine, and its plural confirms this irregular pattern: *le mani* (feminine plural article *le* with masculine plural ending *-i*), not *i mani*.

Sudare sette camicie IDIOMATIC EXPRESSION

(soo-DAH-reh SET-teh kah-MEE-cheh)

To work extremely hard

Sudare sette camicie literally translates as "to sweat seven shirts," and it is used figuratively to describe working very hard, putting in enormous effort, or struggling through a challenging task. The phrase emphasizes physical or mental effort to achieve a goal. For example, a student might say, "*Per superare l'esame ho sudato sette camicie,*" meaning "I worked really hard to pass the exam," or an employee might comment, "*Ho sudato sette camicie per finire il progetto in tempo*" ("I really struggled to finish the project on time"). This idiom originates from the vivid image of someone sweating so much that it would soak through not just one shirt but seven. It exaggerates the effort, making the description dramatic and humorous. You may notice that this exaggeration is typical of Italian expressions, which use visual metaphors to convey emotion and intensity. In modern Italian, ***sudare sette camicie*** can be applied to almost any situation requiring persistence or hard work: studying, physical exercise, managing difficult tasks, or dealing with complicated personal issues. It can also convey admiration for effort and determination. For instance, a coach might praise an athlete, "*Hai sudato sette camicie durante questo allenamento!*" ("You worked incredibly hard during this training!"). The verb *sudare* ("to sweat") must be conjugated according to the tense and subject. For example, in the present continuous, one could say, "*Sto sudando sette camicie*" ("I'm working extremely hard").

Tra il dire e il fare c'è di mezzo il mare PROVERB

(trah eel DEE-reh eh eel FAH-reh cheh dee MEH-tsoh eel MAH-reh)

There is a big difference between saying and doing

Tra il dire e il fare c'è di mezzo il mare literally translates to "between saying and doing there is in the middle the sea." Figuratively, it expresses the idea that it is much easier to talk about doing something than to actually do it. For example, a friend might say, "*Puoi promettere di aiutarmi, ma ricorda che* ***tra il dire e il fare c'è di mezzo il mare***," meaning "You can promise to help me, but remember that saying and doing are very different." Just as crossing the sea is challenging and takes effort, moving from words to action can be difficult and requires commitment. It emphasizes the gap between intentions or plans and real-world execution, reminding people that promises and intentions alone are not enough, they must be followed by action. In modern Italian, this phrase is frequently used to comment on procrastination and unfulfilled promises. It is common in conversations about work, school, personal projects, or life decisions. Its tone can be cautionary or even slightly reproachful, depending on context.

Same Idea, Different Words English has a similar proverb you likely recognize: "Easier said than done." Both expressions highlight the universal truth that intentions must be paired with effort and action, but the Italian version adds a poetic, vivid twist by imagining the obstacle as an entire sea between words and action.

Un sacco NOUN

(oon SAHK-koh)

A lot; Very much

Un sacco literally means "a sack" or "a bag," but figuratively it is used in Italian to express a large quantity or intensity. It is one of the most common informal expressions to say "a lot" or "very much." For example, a person might say, "*Mi piace* ***un sacco*** *questo film*" ("I like this movie a lot"), or "*Ho studiato* ***un sacco*** *per l'esame*" ("I studied very much for the exam"). It can refer to tangible things, like objects, or intangible things, like feelings, effort, or time. This Italian expression originates from the literal image of a sack filled to the top. In everyday life, a sack is often associated with being full and heavy, so ***un sacco*** became a metaphor for abundance or intensity. Its informal, conversational tone makes it ideal for casual conversations among friends and family. ***Un sacco*** can amplify adjectives, verbs, or even other expressions: *Ci divertiremo* ***un sacco*** ("We'll have a lot of fun") or *Ho mangiato* ***un sacco*** ("I ate a lot").

Lots and Loads Other ways to say "a lot" in Italian include *molto* ("very") or *tantissimo* ("very much"). However, ***un sacco*** carries a casual, colloquial tone that is highly common in spoken Italian and immediately understood by all age groups. It adds emphasis in a friendly way, much like "loads" or "tons" in English.

Vivere alla giornata VERB PHRASE

(VEE-veh-reh AHL-lah jor-NAH-tah)

To live day by day

Vivere alla giornata literally translates to "to live by the day," and figuratively it describes an attitude of living in the present, taking life as it comes, and not worrying too much about the future. Italians use it to convey a relaxed, spontaneous approach to life. For example, you might hear someone say, "*Non penso troppo al futuro, preferisco **vivere alla giornata***" ("I don't think too much about the future, I prefer to live day by day"), or a traveler might describe their vacation plan, "*Quest'estate vivremo alla giornata, senza programmi fissi*" ("This summer we'll live day by day, with no fixed plans"). This common phrase captures a balance between enjoying life's moments and coping with uncertainty. It originates from traditional Italian lifestyles, particularly in rural areas, where day-to-day survival and seasonal work shaped the rhythm of life. Over time, it became a metaphor for prioritizing the present, appreciating what one has, and accepting unpredictability. In modern usage, ***vivere alla giornata*** can describe both positive and negative situations. Positively, it evokes freedom, spontaneity, and joy. Negatively, it can suggest irresponsibility or lack of planning, depending on context. For example, a parent might warn a teenager who spends money freely, "*Non puoi sempre **vivere alla giornata***" ("You can't always live day by day").

Further Reading and Listening

Books

***The Penguin Italian Phrasebook* by Jill Norman, Pietro Giorgetti, Daphne Tagg, and Sonia Gallucci**
A compact phrasebook offering essential vocabulary, travel expressions, and practical communication for everyday situations.

***Italian-English Bilingual Visual Dictionary* by DK**
An illustrated dictionary teaching Italian vocabulary through images, labels, and clear English translations.

***Speak Italian: The Fine Art of the Gesture* by Bruno Munari**
This book explores Italian hand gestures, explaining meanings, cultural context, and nonverbal communication essentials.

***Italian Frequency Dictionary—Essential Vocabulary: 2,500 Most Common Italian Words* by Letizia Lorini**
A vocabulary reference listing the 2,500 most frequently used Italian words.

Blogs and Websites

Focus.it

An Italian popular science website with news and articles on science, nature, tech, culture, and environment.

TheItalianExperiment.com

An Italian learning site with short stories, lessons, audio, and simple grammar explanations for different learning levels.

Podcasts

***Italian Grammar Made Easy* by Margherita Berti**

A beginner-friendly podcast explaining Italian grammar concepts with practical examples and real-life usage.

***News in Slow Italian* by Linguistica 360**

An Italian news podcast spoken slowly, combining current events with support for learning the language.

***Giorno per Giorno* by Corriere della Sera**

"Day by Day": A daily Italian news podcast offering concise, clear explanations of current events and major headlines.

***Le scienze nella vita di Tutti i Giorni* by Geopop**

"Science in Everyday Life": An Italian science podcast explaining everyday phenomena in a clear and accessible way, through real-life examples.

About the Author

Margherita Berti, PhD, is the founder of Italian Matters, an online Italian language hub with five million followers across platforms. She holds a PhD in Applied Linguistics and creates digital courses and resources to help learners build real-world Italian fluency. Margherita also hosts the *Italian Grammar Made Easy* podcast and shares language tips through engaging videos and social content.